Wilderness Survival and Knot Tying for Kids

Essential Outdoor Skills and Fun Knotting Techniques for Young Adventurers

Table of Contents

Part 1: Wilderness Survival for Kids

A Comprehensive Guide to Finding Water, Foraging, Shelter Building, and More Essential Skills for Surviving in the Wild

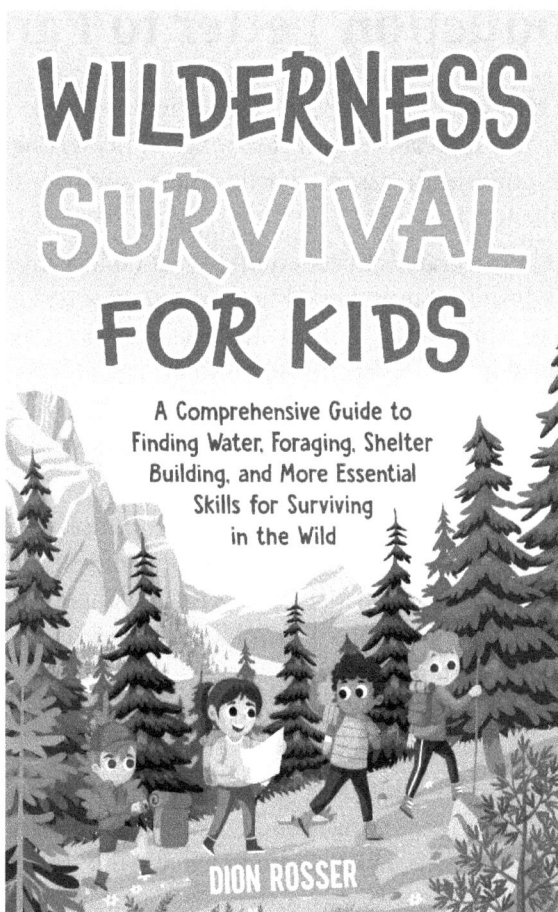

Introduction Letter to Parents

Thank you for choosing this exciting educational resource to add to your children's outdoor education and learning. This engaging book will empower your child with essential wilderness survival skills, all while keeping safety the top priority.

This comprehensive guidebook equips your child with the knowledge and skills needed when journeying in the great outdoors. Covering a range of topics, from preparing for wilderness adventures to handling emergencies and staying safe from wild animals, it serves as an educational tool, fostering a deeper connection to nature while teaching practical survival skills. Through easy-to-follow instructions, children learn valuable teamwork, problem-solving, and self-reliance lessons.

The safety of every child is the central concern. Your child is encouraged to practice these skills responsibly under adult supervision, ensuring a secure and controlled learning environment. While the book encourages outdoor exploration, it emphasizes the importance of staying safe and prepared for unexpected situations.

The book dives deep into various survival skills, including, but not limited to, finding water and wild edibles, starting fires, building shelters, staying safe around wild animals, creating useful tools, handling first aid and emergencies, learning navigation, and exploring additional survival hacks. These skills provide practical knowledge while instilling respect for the natural world and responsibility toward the environment.

Thank you for taking the time to nurture your child's outdoor education. Your child's safety and education are the top priorities. Enjoy this journey of exploration and learning, as there's nothing greater than discovering the wonders of the planet and one's own capabilities!

Introduction Letter to Children

It's great that you have chosen this book to guide you on this wild and wonderful journey. Here, you will learn about staying safe and surviving in the wilderness. You're about to become a true wilderness expert, and this book is your secret roadmap to all the incredible knowledge you need to enjoy the great outdoors safely. You will have so much fun learning some seriously cool stuff.

The first section of this awesome book prepares you for epic wilderness adventures. It's all about being ready for anything and making sure you have the right tools and knowledge to have a blast while staying safe. Then, you'll learn to find clean water and even delicious wild edibles.

That's not all, as the next section teaches you how to start a fire. You'll explore how to build your very own shelter. Whether it's a cozy den or a cool treehouse, you'll know how to create a safe space in the wild.

Guess what? In this book, you'll also learn how to stay safe around amazing wild animals. You'll know how to respect their space and enjoy nature without any worries. You'll be prepared to take action when it comes to first aid and emergencies. You can help in tricky situations and keep everyone safe with the knowledge you'll gain. This book is your guide to let you master navigation, so you'll always find your way back to camp or safety.

Every skill in this book comes with some awesome safety tips. You should follow these rules like they're your treasure map to adventure. So, as you journey through the pages, remember that you're going to be safe, responsible, and – most of all – you will have a ton of fun. What are you waiting for? Get ready to explore, learn, and discover all the amazing things the great outdoors has to offer.

Section 1: Preparing for the Wilderness

If this is your first time experiencing the wilderness, you are right to be excited. This trip will be nothing short of an adventure. You'll get to be in the wild, running around freely, climbing trees, surrounded by animals and greenery, and doing all sorts of thrilling activities that nature offers. To get the most out of your natural escapade, you need to put some thought into the trip's preparations. Safety always comes first, and there is no safer way than being prepared for any surprises and armed with the knowledge of how to act in the face of danger or in an emergency.

It's a good idea to prepare an agenda. Do some research on the place you're going to, what it offers, and how to get there. You'd be surprised how many people reach their destinations only to find out there is an activity they wanted to do but haven't packed the gear needed for it because they didn't know it existed.

Part of preparation is asking others about their previous experiences, like a parent or a friend. Often, people don't learn important details about a situation until they've lived through it, which is a good chance for others to have the experience without the unpleasantness of going through it.

Destination Planning

First things first, where are you going?

First, you need to decide on a destination.

Consider a few things while picking the national park you're heading to. How far is it? Will you need to commute, or will someone drive you? What's the weather going to be like? Is it safe to go without a parent or guardian? What sort of wildlife is there, and what precautions should you take to protect yourself against predators? There are many more questions that you need answers to before embarking on your quest.

Location

After you've picked out the destination, you'll need to research the area as much as you can. Most national parks have websites with information such as hiking trails and camping information. Check whether or not the area you're going to requires a permit to enter and, if so, how to get it.

Pick a place based on how long you're staying and how far you're willing to hike. If you'll be staying for a weekend, it's best to pick a site close to home so you don't spend half the trip on the road.

Take into consideration what you want to see, such as lakes, mountains, waterfalls, etc. You should also base your destination choice on the activities you want to do during your stay.

Check online for the maps of the trails and pick the one you want to tackle. Mark the campsites and water sources on the map in case you run low on supplies. Make sure you have GPS and a compass active on your phone, along with the physical map and compass. Save the locations on your phone for further reference while walking the trail.

If you're not going with a parent or a group, make sure that there is someone at home who knows where you'll be and how long you'll be gone. Set up check-in timings with them so they know you're okay.

Weather and Timing

Based on the time of year, you should be able to note the weather in the area unless it's in a different region. In that case, you'll need to check the forecast and the historic weather fluctuations.

Remember, in shaded areas, the temperatures drop quite low at night, so you need to pack your clothes accordingly.

Look for sun exposure, hours of daylight, and footwear information before you head out.

You'll need special boots and gear to move freely if there is snow. You'll also need to check if the trail is open because some trails close down during the snow season as a safety measure.

If you're going up a mountain, the temperature goes down the higher you go, and so does the oxygen level.

Summer trips are known for having the best weather, but this is also the most crowded time of year.

If you're a novice in camping, it is advised not to spend too much time on your first trip. 2 or 3 days is a good start to get the lay of the land and see how you like it, along with what works and what doesn't work for you.

The Company You Keep

Hiking is the perfect opportunity for bonding and getting to know others properly. People usually reveal their strengths and weaknesses when faced with adversity. They also come together and rely on one another when there is a challenge and no one else is around.

If you can't find someone to join you, you can post in the local trail discussion groups that you're looking for someone to hike with. Just make sure you inform your parents and give them the details of the person coming with you if they're not joining you.

Having company with you is not just for fun and games; it is preferred for safety reasons. If something unexpected is to happen, an injury, you get lost, or you lose some of your supplies, it's good to have someone along with backup to save the day.

When traveling with family, friends, or a group, the pace by which you move will be adjusted to accommodate the slowest person in the group. No one gets left behind.

Having someone along can also help reduce the weight you're carrying by sharing a tent, a kettle, and food.

Permit and Transportation

The more famous and popular the trail, the more likely you'll need to book a permit in advance. Some permits are immediate, but others may require months to secure a date. The popular spots employ *lottery-based permits*, meaning you must enroll months before your planned trip and wait to see if you're chosen.

Depending on the location, if you can't get a permit, there is sometimes an option to get a walk-up permit right before you hit the trail.

Not all trails allow backcountry camping (spread-out camping), which could mean you'll need to book separate campgrounds for the duration of your trip.

All the information you'll need on the permits should be found online, especially if it's a national or state forest.

As for the way you're going, that will depend on the distance. If it's a long drive or requires a flight, you're probably traveling with a camping group or your parents.

If you're somewhere nearby and safe enough to head out alone, you'll need someone to drop you off or take the shuttle.

Itinerary, Budget, and Rules

If you're going on a long trip, you need to plan for it.
https://unsplash.com/photos/six-white-sticky-notes–
1_RZL8BGBM?utm_content=creditShareLink&utm_medium=referral&utm_source=unsplash

Planning day-to-day activities is usually associated with longer trips. You don't usually need a detailed plan if the trip is only one or two days.

Your plan should include how far you'll walk every day, where you are camping, and what activities you'll do each day.

Long trips should include a rest day or an extra day if you don't have enough time to fit everything in.

Examine your supplies and food and see how much it'll cost to refill and buy anything you need. Also, consider that there may be transportation and permit costs.

When researching the park, pay attention to the rules and regulations posted. These rules keep you safe and give you the best experience possible during your stay. Look out for areas you need to stay clear of due to wild animals, a dangerous terrain that's been warned against, or a river known to have a strong current.

Be mindful of your surroundings, and always remember that you need to leave the area in the same, if not a better, condition than when you arrived. This means no littering, no cutting greenery, or damaging anything in the campsite, including the warning and direction signs.

Animals and Insects

In most areas, you don't need to worry about encountering any dangerous predators. The most likely appearances you'll encounter on your trip are raccoons, mice, and any form of rodents. However, you must pay attention to the warning signs at the park entrance or the start of the terrain.

In some areas, you may come across cougars, bears, or venomous snakes; in that case, the safest bet is to avoid that plot altogether.

If that is not an option, you must educate yourself on the safety measures to avoid injury or a life-threatening chase.

For example, if you're camping in a bear habitat, learn what to do if you come face to face with one and what type of bears are present. Also, learn how to store your food to keep it away from the bear, like using bear canisters.

You can count on meeting a few insects, so pack insect-repellent clothing and environment-friendly sprays to keep yourself bite-free.

You can also use a sleeping net as a hammock and mosquito nets during meal times to preserve your sanity.

Another way known among backpackers to keep mosquitos away is to wear rain gear.

Packing Your Outdoor Adventure Kit

If you're new to this, it's easy to be a little overwhelmed by the packing process. You don't want to over-pack to prevent walking around with an unnecessarily heavy load, and you don't want to play it so cool that you forget necessary items.

Each trip is different in terms of length, level of difficulty, location, and activities. However, there are some essential items you'll need to have on you for a successful trip:

Necessities

A compass is a necessary item when going to the wilderness.

- Compass and a map (in case your phone dies and you need to figure out your way back or your next stopping point)
- Pocket flashlight for nighttime
- Multi-tool or a Swiss army knife
- Emergency blanket
- Tent
- Water flask and water filters for when you get to the water source
- Tools to start a fire, like a magnifying glass, lighter, matches, and lighter fluid
- A small bag to hold small items in your supplies
- First aid kit
- Sleeping bag
- Environment-friendly toiletries
- Trowel
- Repair tape
- If possible, a satellite phone, in case you're in an area with no bars

Clothing

- Hiking boots
- Hoodie or fleece
- Jacket
- Long underwear
- Waterproof attire
- Pairs of socks covering the period of the trip
- Hiking pants, shorts, and shirt
- Headwear for cold and hot weather
- Sandals for moving around the camp
- Sunglasses and sunscreen

Food

It's important to have a kettle in the wilderness.
Photo by laura adai on Unsplash https://unsplash.com/photos/stainless-steel-kettle-on-brown-wooden-table-JJHhMAD0wCU

- Lightweight stove and fuel
- Pots and utensils
- Sponge and soap (not to eat, to clean the pots with!)
- Spork, cup, and a bowl for each person

- Water, at least 32 ounces, should be on you at all times, along with the kit to purify water.
- Kettle
- Obviously, *food!*

    Keep with you between 1.5 to 2.5 pounds of dry food per person. The effort you exert, and considering the speed you're moving, the elevation, and the distance, will drastically affect the amount you need to eat. Some people recommend that if you're new to backpacking, it won't hurt to over-pack food until you can ascertain your consumption and also in case of an emergency.
- Protein and energy bars, dried fruit, granola, and jerky.

Miscellaneous

- Equipment specific to the activities you want to partake in. A bicycle, if there is biking terrain. Kayak, if you're into rowing down river streams. Walking poles for hiking. If you're going during the snow season, then ski equipment and swim trunks, or if you're going swimming in a lake or river.
- Electronics, phones, cameras, headphones, iPod, and battery-based chargers.
- Have some fun items on you, like astrology books, games, stories, a journal or your sketchbook, and a coloring kit.

Emergency Tools and First Aid

Prepare yourself for the outdoors with first aid and emergency training. Being aware of when you are in a tight situation and how to act accordingly and appropriately can be the difference between ending up with a band-aid and being airlifted to a hospital.

Signaling

There are a lot of signals used in survival training. All rescue personnel are aware of the meanings and the different nature of each one, making this tool one of the most effective in alerting the authorities that you need help.

These signals include fire, flashing lights, mirrors, flags, colored markers, and whistles.

As most search and rescue uses helicopters, aircraft, and maybe drones, it's a good idea to form your signals in an open area so they're easily discovered.

For instance, if you form three fires in a triangle, this can be interpreted as a distress signal, especially if a drone or a helicopter is flying by. Make sure your fires are carefully banked to prevent setting the surrounding shrubbery on fire.

You can also use mirrors to alert people on planes or from a long distance from your location. They are hard to miss when angled properly with the sun or using a flashlight.

You can use a strobe light at night to alert those nearby in the camping area. You can also generate smoke during the day from fire using organic materials.

Another way to send a signal is to use rocks, logs, and bright-colored clothing by laying them down on the ground and spelling out the word S.O.S. These signals are clear to any airborne craft.

First Aid

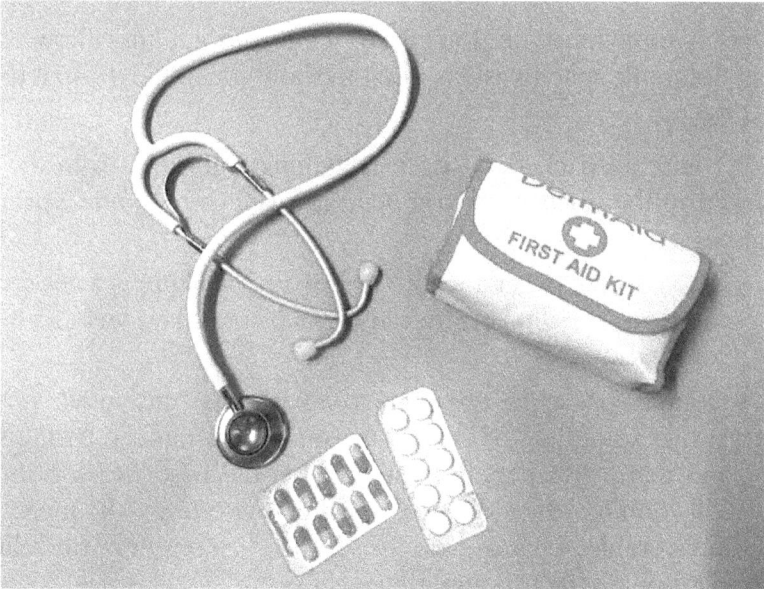

Having a first aid kit and being able to use it are two different things.
https://unsplash.com/photos/a-bag-of-pills-a-stethoscope-and-a-first-aid-kit-ZyxNWi3JClo?utm_content=creditShareLink&utm_medium=referral&utm_source=unsplash

First aid doesn't just include the bandages and antiseptic you have on you. A primary component of survival is your attitude. You need to stay calm and collected. Do not let your panic grab the steering wheel. Use STOP, which stands for Sit, Think, Observe, and Plan.

Implement logic, assess your situation, and determine what you need to safely escape it.

It is important to detail the medical equipment you'll need. If you have a specific condition, like diabetes or IBS, make sure you have the medication for that. If you have allergies or suspect you may be allergic to anything in the wilderness, have antihistamines with you just in case. These should be packed safely in waterproof containers, which are kept safely on you at all times.

Don't forget to include the basics, like dressings for small cuts and bruises. If there are any items in the kit you've never used before, you need to go over how to safely administer these items.

You can protect yourself against hypothermia by using a space blanket at night. Make sure your gear is labeled, and you have a family picture on you with your address written on the back and a contact number so that if you're lost or lose your things, whoever finds them has a place to start looking from.

If there is something you don't understand or don't know how or when to use it, do not hesitate to ask an adult to show you and explain it to you.

Final Sweep

Once you're all packed, go over everything you have, from the things you packed to the documents you need to make sure you're not missing anything.

- Lift your bag to get a feel of its heaviness. There is a good chance you won't need that extra can of beans once you feel its weight on your back.
- Double-check the weather to avoid any unwanted surprises. While some people love going out in the rain or during storms and damp weather, this may not be the best idea for someone still finding their footing in the wilderness. If there is an unfavorable change in the forecast, consider canceling or postponing the trip until things get better.
- Share your plans with people you trust, like your parents, guardians, or close friends. If you have a satellite phone, provide them with the number. Also, leave your details in several places within your gear in case you need to be found.
- Make sure you have an evacuation route marked in case of an emergency or unforeseen weather.

Section 2: Water and Wild Edibles

Staying hydrated and well-nourished while exploring the outdoors is vital to enjoying the experience. You won't be having fun if you feel too weak to move or partake in activities. A big part of Boy Scouts' training is finding clean water and edible food on your own in the wild. Why, may you ask? Well, there are several scenarios where you may need this training.

These scenarios may involve under-packing your food, losing some of it, or being overly generous when sharing it with the forest critters. You could get lost, or a bear steals your food.

In both cases, you need to be armed with the knowledge of how to keep yourself alive by acquiring food and water from natural sources.

Remember, just because you're about to learn how to gather water and food from the wild doesn't mean you should forgo preparing and packing for your potential needs.

You should only resort to natural sources if you absolutely have to.

Water

Assume you lost your water flask, it broke, or you drank all the water you have and still have a long way to go. Keep calm, and don't panic. Survival depends on decisions made in the first few minutes of realizing an emergency. Making a decision out of fear will only make matters worse.

Don't worry about losing your water flask; make a way to tote it or keep up with it. Survival is all about making decisions in an emergency.

Start by monitoring your body's response to the environment. Is it cool where you are? Are you sweating profusely? Is your body losing water quickly, or can you last a while longer without a water source?

Now that you've settled down and assessed your situation, you can start the search for drinking water. The three primary types of water you'll be looking for are surface water, like rivers and lakes, groundwater from springs, and rainwater.

Pay Attention

Remember that water collected from lakes, rivers, or plant condensation must be filtered and purified. It is not safe to drink water straight from the source. However, if faced with a life-or-death situation, then you'll probably have no choice besides biting the bullet and taking that risk. Just be aware that any water you drink that hasn't been through a filtration process will most likely have bacteria. Also, be mindful that some techniques used in collecting water make it safer to drink than others.

Remember, it is always better to target running water whenever you can. The flow of the river or stream makes it hard for bacteria to manifest and spread. So, your number one choice should be small streams and underground reservoirs. Rivers come in next, but note that they may carry pollution from upstream. Always collect water as close to the upstream as possible where the current is fast. Lakes and ponds are an acceptable choice. However, they have a higher chance of bacterial presence because of the stagnant water.

Just because the water is clear doesn't mean it's safe to drink. Look for signs of life. If there aren't any around, not even algae, do not drink it. It won't be safe. Also, avoid water sources where rats are present.

Rivers and Streams

This is an excellent exercise to train your ninja senses. Stand perfectly still, close your eyes, and listen. Water sounds can sometimes be heard even if the source is pretty far away.

Now, open your eyes and try to locate any animal tracks. Although a damper on camping, a swarm of insects indicates nearby water. A bird's flight path also leads to bodies of water. So, keep your eyes peeled and your ears to the ground.

Take a look around you and notice the terrain you're on. Water runs downwards, so follow any valleys you see and look out for ravines or ditches. If you arrive at low ground, you're likely to find water.

Underground Water

Underground water signs can include dried river beds and wet dirt. Notice if there are any signs of green vegetation, like shrubs, which are common around water sources. Look for animals assembling in one area. This usually indicates water is below the surface.

Start digging until you feel the sand or dirt getting wet, then wait until the water seeps into the hole.

Be sure to purify the water you gather from the hole you dug.

Rain Water and Morning Dew

Rain is probably one of the safest and easiest methods of collecting water, and as long as you're not in a heavily industrialized area (where rain turns acidic), you're probably safe. You can use a tarp, tree leaves, or even your own clothing to gather the rain. The water gathered from this source is usually pure and needs minimal purification.

You can also find some droplets trapped between the leaves and stems of plants following the rain.

You may think that morning dew is a very small amount of water that won't make that much of a difference. However, these small droplets can easily add up to substantial amounts of drinking water. This is especially true in grassy areas.

Be sure to start collecting early in the morning before the sun rises and the water evaporates. You can tie a cloth around your ankles or wrists and walk around in a tall grassy area. The dew will be caught in the cloth, and then you can wring out the water into your container.

Another source similar to the morning dew is the *Sphagnum* moss. These plants grow close to the ground and are often located in damp areas, under the shade of trees away from the light. The moss collects water quite well, and you can retrieve it by pulling apart a clump and squeezing it to release the liquid.

Snow and Ice

Snow and ice are abundantly available in areas of high altitude and colder weather. As straightforward as this sounds, there are a few things to be cautious about.

Don't ever drink ice or snow in huge quantities all at once. This has the potential to lower your body temperature drastically and suddenly and can cause hypothermia.

Melt the ice first. Place it in a pan; add more when the first batch has melted.

Purifying the Water

- Boiling - A common method is using a cloth to filter out any large bits of sediment and then boiling the water. Bacteria cannot withstand high temperatures, so 10 minutes over the fire should do it.

However, you need a container of some sort to start a fire. If you can't find a traditional container, use a plastic bottle, tin can, aluminum can, glass jar, or a large shell. Now, you might worry that the plastic bottle will melt, but if you fill it to the brim and tightly close it, the lack of air should stop the damage. You can also suspend it in the air above the fire.

If you can't start a fire, place the water in the sun in a clear flask to kill the bacteria.

- **Filtration Pumps:** These pumps are filters you can find in any camping store. The water passes over a ceramic or charcoal filter that treats any impurities in it, sometimes using chemicals as well. The end result is pure, drinkable water when you're stuck outdoors.

- **Purification Tablets and Drops:** This is a simple and cheap way to clean water collected from the wild. All you have to do is add a couple of tablets or drops to your water container, wait for 20 minutes, and voila! You have drinking water. The tablets usually contain iodine, chlorine, potassium, and permanganate. You can also add powdered mixes to mask the taste.

  Always consult a doctor before using these, as they may cause medical issues if you are sensitive to any of the components or if you have a specific medical condition. Also, the chlorine used to purify the water is different from the tablets used for the pool, so don't use those.

- **Use Plants:** Some plants in the wild are purifying agents. However, you must familiarize yourself with them because a simple mistake can have dire consequences. These plants include xylem, rice and coconuts, cilantro, fruit and banana peels, Oregon grape, and many others.

  Soak these plants in your water and seal them together. The plants will naturally work on clearing and purifying your water.

- **Sedimentation:** This is a no-brainer. If you place your water in a container and leave it stagnant, the impurities are bound to sink to the bottom. All you need to do is scoop the water up without disturbing it so it doesn't get mixed together again.

Water Containers

When choosing the containers to store your water in, you'll find there are quite a few options. If you're carrying a lot of luggage and don't want to add to the weight, a handy and cheap option is plastic water bottles, though they don't offer much when it comes to durability.

If you want a sturdier option, go for water jugs. They're a bit heavier but more environmentally friendly than plastic bottles. Remember not to leave plastic bottles in a natural environment.

You can always use specialized containers. These are tailored to the camping crowd, easy to carry, and durable, but they cost a little bit extra.

However, if you consider how long they last, you'll find that they are a good investment.

Wild Edibles

One of the first golden rules of gathering food from Mother Nature is to only eat what you know is safe. If you can't identify it, don't eat it.

The process of locating sustenance from the wild is called foraging. Many campers and wildlife enthusiasts rely on this process for food and sometimes medicine, especially if they stay outdoors for long periods.

Specialists implement edibility tests to be sure that what they're eating is not toxic or poisonous.

Consider having a field guide of the area with details of the wild edibles and the poisonous and toxic plants.

So, how does one forage?

Edible Options

Humans can go a long time without eating, so don't risk it unless you're sure of what you're putting in your body. However, there are some go-to safe options to boost your energy levels if need be.

- **Berries**

Mulberries are edible 99% of the time.

Berries are a really good source of carbs, vitamins, and fiber. Look for the ones packed together tightly, like raspberries and mulberries (also known as aggregate berries). Those are edible 99% of the time. It is recommended to do an edibility test regardless of how certain you are about what you're eating.

Blue, black, and purple berries are around 90% edible. Orange and red berries are 50% edible, and green, white, and yellow berries are 10% edible, so stay away from that last one and do not take the risk, not even with an edibility test.

• Greens

There are obvious options, like fruit and vegetables. However, if you can't find those, your next best bet is weed. Many weed-like plants, like dandelion, clover, chicory, cattail, lamb's quarters, amaranth, nettles, purslane, sorrel, and mustard, are edible.

A highly recommended option is onions. Just make sure it looks and smells like an onion. If it doesn't, put it down. Also, anything that smells like almonds but doesn't look like almonds is a red flag.

• Insects

Believe it or not, insects contain seven times the amount of protein found in ground beef!

If you are forced down that road, the safe options to try are earthworms, ants (boil those first in case they're fire ants), crickets, grasshoppers (remove legs and wings), and mealworms.

• Birds and Snakes

Pigeons are safe to eat.

If you're up for it and know how to catch birds, go for it. Pigeons, crows, or seagulls are all safe to eat.

With snakes, though, it's a bit tricky. Stay away from any venomous ones. If you can't 100% tell if it is poisonous, do not attempt to catch it.

- **Marine Life**

   Small fish in lakes or rivers, such as isopods, freshwater crustaceans, and oysters, are edible.

Poisonous Plants

Examples of poisonous plants are poison hemlock, foxglove, water hemlock, poison oak, or poison ivy. When you're out in the wild, you must be able to identify the marks of a dangerous plant. Some of these marks are easy to spot without the help of a field guide.

- **Waxy Leaves**: The wax present on the leaves of some plants can be a simple indicator that it has a protective layer that retains water. However, it can also indicate that this plant is toxic. Anything with leaves resembling parsley, dill, or parsnip is probably poisonous.

- **Milky Sap**: This is a substance that oozes out of the plant when the stem breaks. It can cause skin irritation and allergic reactions.

- **Mushrooms:** You need to be able to identify mushrooms with absolute certainty. Morel, oyster, and chanterelle mushrooms are safe and edible. If you can't name it, don't pick it. Don't be tempted by the fungi growing on trees or on the ground.

- **Umbrella-Shaped Flower Clusters**: Most of these umbrella-shaped flowers are toxic and should be avoided at all costs.

- **Fine Hairs and Spines:** Plants with these characteristics usually have a defense mechanism against predators. In this case, the predator is you. A lot of these hairs can sting and burn once you touch them.

- **Trust the Taste**: If you taste the plant and are *struck with a bitter or soapy taste*, spit it out immediately. Poisonous plants always taste bad.

- **Bright Colors**: Insects, plants, marine life, whatever it is, stay away from anything with bright colors.

Edibility Test

There is a way to test plants when you're not 100% sure whether or not they are edible (like orange berries).

- **Rule out the Poisonous Traits**: Go through the previously mentioned poison indicators before examining them further.

- **Skin Test:** Rub a piece of the plant on your forearm or outer lip. Wait for about 15 minutes to see if there is a reaction.

- **Taste Test:** If there is no skin reaction, taste the same bit you tested on your skin. Wait for another 5 minutes.

- **Take a Bigger Taste Test:** If there is no reaction and you don't taste any bitterness, soapy flavor, or almond flavor or feel any numbness, take a bigger bite, the size of a teaspoon, and then wait 8 hours.

- **Eat a Bit More:** If you're still not suffering from any digestive issues, eat another teaspoon and wait another 8 hours. If nothing happens, you can consider that part of the plant edible in the state in which you performed the taste test (raw, cooked, dried).

- **Be Careful:** Be mindful, and use your common sense. If you're unsure what you're eating, don't take an unnecessary risk. The human body can survive 30 days without food and three without water.

Many of the edible options have poisonous twins. Sometimes, the fruit is edible, but the stems and leaves aren't. Just because one part is safe doesn't mean all of it is. Only eat the bit you tested and are sure it is edible.

Section 3: Starting a Fire

Not the arson kind! Burning things to a crisp is the only drawback of fire. If you take care, it doesn't destroy or spread and will prove to be one of your most useful allies in the wilderness. Fire can cook your food, decontaminate your water, signal for help, keep wild animals at bay, and provide warmth and light. Armed with the knowledge of starting a fire, your chances of survival in the wilderness rise significantly. Furthermore, you don't need to pack anything extra to start a fire in the woods. All the required tools will be available in nature, but it always helps to keep a match or a lighter handy.

Starting a fire can help you cook and decontaminate water.
https://unsplash.com/photos/bonfire-in-forest-during-night-time-

Key Elements

As you may know, fire is the result of the combustion process. It is a reaction between three key elements: fuel, oxygen, and heat. It is called the "fire triangle".

- **Fuel**

    Fuel can be anything that combusts upon the addition of heat. Materials like paper, wood, clothes, certain liquids and gasses, rubber, etc. can be used as fuel. Materials that don't burn are not considered fuel. For instance, an iron rod will melt after adding a certain amount of heat but not combust.

- **Oxygen**

    Oxygen is a naturally occurring element that is available all around us. Fuel burns due to a reaction with oxygen. Without the presence of oxygen in the atmosphere, you cannot light a fire, even if you have the other two parts of the triangle. Therefore, you cannot start a fire on the moon because there is no oxygen, but you definitely can in the Earth's wilderness.

- **Heat**

    Just as oxygen helps you survive, heat helps fire thrive. You simply cannot start a fire without the presence of heat. You cannot just use the heat from the atmosphere, however. For practical purposes, you will need an ignition source that will produce a spark of heat at a much higher temperature, like a match.

Fire Safety Precautions

Imagine that you successfully lit a fire in a forest. You gave it enough fuel to last for hours and left it unattended as you snuggled in your blanket for a good night's sleep. Over time, the dry leaves near the burning fuel catch fire, quickly spreading all around. The crackling of combustion and the excess heat wake you up. Due to the lack of a water source nearby, you frantically think about what to do next. At a complete loss, you run from the place and out of the woods. Eventually, the nearby trees will catch fire, too, and in a matter of hours, the entire forest will be burning with fierce intensity.

Don't let this eventuality frighten you from starting a fire in the wilderness. There are several ways to avoid the drawbacks of fires. Take these few good precautions.

- **Dig a Fire Pit**

  Most campsites already have fire pits in specific places. If there isn't one, feel free to pick up a shovel and dig, as long as campfires are allowed. Choose an open area with no trees around or above. Are you bang in the middle of the forest? Pick a spot where the nearest tree branches are far above the ground. Sweep a few feet of the area clear. Make sure there aren't any leaves or combustible materials around. Then, start digging the pit until it is roughly eight inches deep.

- **Water Source**

  It is recommended to start a fire near a water source, like a river or a lake, so you can readily douse the flames if something other than the pit's contents catches fire. If you are far from a water source, keep a bucket full of water or a fire blanket on hand.

- **Place Rocks around the Fire**

  Despite the above two precautions, there is still a chance for the fire to spread. To minimize that chance, place rocks around the pit in a circle, enclosing any gaps with smaller stones.

Identifying and Collecting Suitable Firewood/Fuel

You can purchase firewood from a coal shop or a furniture store, but carrying it all the way to the spot isn't exactly feasible. Many campsites are equipped with firewood and other fuel sources. Do you want an authentic wilderness experience instead? Identify the right type of fuel in the vicinity and collect it yourself. Whatever you collect, make sure it's dry. Wet stuff doesn't catch fire. It's stubborn that way.

- Look for fallen twigs or branches, especially in a place where there are a lot of trees.
- Cut down low-hanging tree branches.
- Peel off tree barks that are already jutting out.
- In stony, mountainous regions, you may find firewood underneath rocks.

- Branches from a dead tree are devoid of moisture, perfect for kindling a fire. Its rotting part provides a tinder, and you can use the trunk of a fallen tree as fuel logs.
- Dry leaves and pine needles are perfect sources of tinder.
- You may need to climb a tree to find dry firewood in wet conditions. The sun's rays evaporate moisture quickly from the topmost branches.

Arranging the Firewood

You can simply dump the fuel into the fire pit and light it up. However, it won't be efficient and may fizzle out after a few minutes. You don't want all the hours you spent collecting firewood to go to waste. There are several ways to arrange firewood for efficient combustion. Here are three of the most common arrangements.

- **Teepee Fire**

A teepee fire.

If you have been camping for a while, you may know what a teepee (also spelled as tipi) tent looks like. It's a conical shelter held together with wooden poles and covered with a cloth. Your teepee fire will be structurally similar, except made of logs, branches, twigs, and tinder.

1. Place the tinder at the center of the pit.
2. Cover it with small branches in the form of a teepee tent. Grab a few branches in one palm, hold the top, and arrange the bottom around the tinder in a cone.
3. Finally, place the fuel logs around the branches in a cone. Leave enough space between each log to maintain constant airflow.

• Lean-to Fire

As the name suggests, a lean-to fire leans onto something (in this case, a log or a tree trunk). It doesn't need a fire pit and can be kindled even in strong wind. The trunk provides excellent cover.

1. Position the log or the trunk perpendicular to the wind direction.
2. Place the tinder so that the log face protects it from the wind.
3. Arrange twigs and branches on top of it, with one end leaning on the log.
4. Add bigger logs to provide better cover.

• Log Cabin Fire

This is a more robust type of arrangement. It protects your fire from the wind and provides a base for you to place a kettle or a bowl for cooking. The contraption is square-shaped, with an opening at the base to light the tinder.

1. Place the tinder or kindling in a bunch on the floor.
2. Arrange two logs horizontally opposite each other. They must be of the same width.
3. Place two more logs on top at a right angle to each. Make sure the tinder within is visible from the top.
4. Similarly, place two more logs at a right angle to the second base. You may construct another story the same way.

Fire-Starting Methods

Once you have dug a fire pit, taken all the precautions, collected the right fuel (tinder, twigs, logs, etc.), and arranged them in your preferred style, it's time to start a fire. The easiest and safest way is to strike a match and drop it on the tinder/kindling at the base. Don't try to light the covering branches or logs. They will take a long time to catch fire, and you will end up wasting several matchsticks.

If you use a lighter instead, you must be very careful since you cannot just drop it on the tinder. Never lower the lighter from the top. When the tinder catches fire, it will burn your hand. Approach from the sides. In a teepee fire, you won't be able to access the tinder easily. You must remove the branches and logs from a small section to reach it with your lighter. With lean-to and log cabin fires, there is enough space on the sides to get your lighter near the tinder.

Did you forget to pack both matches and lighter? No sweat. Here are a few other innovative yet safe ways to start a fire.

• **Magnifying Glass**

This is probably the most exciting way to start a fire. Remember the time you used a magnifying glass to focus the sun's rays and heat things up (bowl of water or a piece of paper) just for fun? That is exactly how you can light the tinder.

A magnifying glass can help you start a fire.

Hold the magnifying glass so the sun's rays converge on the tinder. Make as small a point as possible. Within a few minutes, the tinder will begin to smoke, and a few more seconds later, a visible flame will burst into life. As you may have figured out, you can use this technique only during the day under sufficient sunlight, not in the dark of the night.

• **Batteries**

This is an old-fashioned way of starting a fire. You will need a battery with both terminals on one side (not easily available today, hence old-fashioned). You will also need to buy steel wool from a convenience store. Rub the battery terminals on the wool. Make sure you are holding a good thick stack. Otherwise, you may burn your hand. As you rub the terminals on the steel wool, you'll create a spark that will light up the wool. Drop it on the tinder and blow gently on it. After a few seconds, a blazing fire will start.

• **Flint and Steel**

Did you know that flint and steel were first used to start a fire as far back as the 11th century? All you need is a flint rock (usually found near a river), a char cloth (a piece of cloth made of charcoal), and a steel knife. This method will need adult supervision.

Place the char cloth on the flint and hold them together near the edge. Strike the cloth with the knife blade far away from your fingers. After a few good strikes, the cloth will catch fire. Drop it onto the tinder and blow.

Tending the Fire

After starting the fire, you cannot leave it as is. It will burn bright initially, but the intensity will reduce as time passes until it completely dies down. You need to tend the fire occasionally to keep it burning for a long time. Tending simply means that you should place more firewood on it. Add kindling materials like twigs and sticks.

Putting out the Fire

The most important step in starting a fire is being able to put it out. You don't want your camping spot to go up in flames. Admittedly, if you keep the fire untended and leave the spot, it may fizzle out after a while, but there is a high chance it will spread to the surrounding area. However, you can't just pour a bucket full of water on it and leave. You need to ensure that the fire is indeed extinguished. It's a three-step process:

1. Fill your water bucket to the brim and drain it on the burning tinder.
2. Scoop up a handful of soil from the ground and drop it on the doused area. A shovel is recommended for this purpose.
3. Hold your hands (palms facing down) over the pit.

Are you feeling the heat? Then the fire hasn't completely gone out. Stir the residue with a long stick to locate any burning embers. Then, repeat the three-step process again and again until you cannot feel the heat. At this point, ask an adult to touch the ashen, wet residue to be sure the fire has been extinguished. If it's hot, you will need to repeat the three-step process.

That's not all. Follow the "leave no trace" principle. Scatter the ashes in the surrounding area or sweep them off into a corner of the clearing. Remove the stones from around the pit and cover it with soil. Only then will you have successfully put out the fire.

Section 4: Shelter Building

From the basic necessities of wilderness survival, you have already taken care of two. You have packed the right clothes for the adventure and learned how to find food and water to cook on your fire. It's time to tackle the third and final necessity, building a shelter.

The primary use of a wilderness shelter is to protect yourself from the elements. You don't have to construct a log cabin or a fully-fledged house with a lock. You are out in the wilderness with a group of children or adults, so you don't have to worry about thieves. All you need is a roof on your head and makeshift walls on the sides to shield yourself from wind, rain, snow, and heat.

A tent will add to your heavy baggage.
https://www.pexels.com/photo/camping-dome-tent-near-a-body-of-water-2582818/

While you can carry a tent with you, it will only add to your already heavy baggage. Even collapsible tents are bulky and require a lot of space. Wouldn't creating your own shelter from materials readily available in the wilderness would be less cumbersome? Plus, it will be a whole lot of fun!

Shelter Essentials

You don't need a tent to build a proper tent-like shelter. All you need is a tarp and a rope. The rest of the essentials can be found in a natural environment. A rope is a necessary component of your wilderness kit. It has many uses, from shelter building to climbing up or down steep inclines. A tarp, on the other hand, is almost exclusively used for shelter building. Don't want to add it to your burden? Perfectly understandable. You can still make a shelter entirely out of things from the wild. You will need:

- A long, thick tree branch or a log
- Around 20 similar-length branches that are smaller than the main branch
- Lots and lots of dry leaves or pine needles as cover

Why Use a Tarp, Dry Leaves, or Pine Needles?

When building a shelter, you should ensure protection against all elements. The weather may be unpredictable in the wild. There may be scorching heat for one hour, followed by a dense cloud and a deluge of rain the next. If you plan to climb to the top of a mountain, you may even experience stormy winds and incessant snowfall.

A tarp acts as the perfect shelter against all elements. It won't let rain or snow get to you, it will protect you from the burning heat, and if it has been tied properly, it will remain stable in the wind.

A tarp shelters you from all elements.

Dry leaves are an ideal protection against extreme heat and cold. They keep the inside of your shelter cool as a cucumber in hot weather and warm as sunbeams on a chilly winter night. Rain won't be a problem if you have enough leaf layers stacked on top of each other. In a downpour, your shelter will remain as dry as if it hadn't rained at all!

Furthermore, you don't need to carry a camping bed or an air mattress with you. Multiple layers of dry leaves stacked within the shelter provide enough ground elevation and comfort. Pine needles have the same advantages as dry leaves.

Building Different Types of Shelters

Building a shelter out of naturally available materials is a lot like creating different types of fire arrangements, as you learned in the previous chapter. The easiest types of shelters to build are the lean-to and log cabin tents.

• Lean-to Shelter

Drawing of a lean-to shelter.
https://commons.wikimedia.org/wiki/File:Field-expedient_lean-to_and_fire_reflector.jpg

You may remember that a lean-to type of fire consists of several branches propped up against a big log. The method of constructing this type of shelter is similar, but you also need to prop the big log up against a tree for better elevation.

1. Find a strong log or tree trunk a little longer than your height.

2. Pick a tree with a strong branch near the ground.

3. Rest one end of the log against the branch and let the other end fall to the ground. It will look like the hypotenuse of a right-angled triangle.

4. Place one end of the similar-length branches on the log, one beside the other, and let the other end rest on the ground. Do this only on one side of the log and leave the other side open. It will make a sort of slanted cave.

5. Place a large bunch of leaves or pine needles on the ground inside the shelter. Make sure there are enough by checking that your body doesn't touch the ground when you lie on them.

6. Place more leaves or pine needles on the branches so that not a single ray of sunlight falls into the cave from that side.

Pro Tip: you can keep warm at night in your lean-to shelter by starting a fire a couple of feet ahead of the open side.

• Log Cabin Shelter

This is more of a bed than a shelter, but it is extremely effective. Do you remember the log cabin fire in the previous chapter? The method of constructing this shelter is similar. You will need a large pile of logs and branches, along with a big bunch of pine needles.

1. Pick a spot under the shade of a tree.
2. Place two logs parallel to each other at a distance of a little more than your height.
3. Add two long logs or branches on top of the base logs so they are perpendicular, and the distance between them is a little more than your breadth.
4. Add two more sets of logs to complete the structure.
5. Fill the base of this makeshift log cabin with pine needles. Make sure it's comfortable to lie on.
6. Once you're lying down, ask your friend or an adult to cover your body with more pine needles. Leave your face uncovered.

You will be fast asleep in this ultra-comfy shelter within minutes! You can also replace the pine needles with dry leaves if you want.

• Tarp Shelter

A tarp tent isn't the all-natural shelter you want during your wilderness adventure, but it is the fastest to build, and it has the capability of protecting you against all elements. You may know what a tarp shelter looks like. It's usually an inverted V suspended on a rope and affixed to the ground with more ropes. Where there are ropes, there are knots. You should learn two basic types of knots to be able to build a tarp shelter.

• **Taut Line Hitch**: It's mostly used to tie the tarp ends to hooks or trees. (pictures showing each step of the taut line hitch knot)

• **Running Bowline:** It's used to hang the ridgelines to trees.

Ideally, you can use a taut line hitch to tie up the entire tent, but learning a few more knots doesn't hurt! The long ropes on the tarp may become loose over time. Try tying a Prusik knot near the middle.

Follow these steps to build the perfect tarp shelter.

1. A tarp is generally available as a square. If it isn't, cut it into that shape.

2. A hole in each corner will be present as well. If there isn't, punch an inch-wide hole.

3. Find two trees a few feet apart (ideally, a little longer than the length of your tarp). You will build your shelter between them.

4. Connect the two trees with a rope at a height of a couple of inches more than half your tarp. You will be using a running bowline knot on the two ends.

5. Place the tarp over the rope so that it goes through the midpoints of the tarp's sides.

6. Tie a rope through each hole of the four corners with a taut line hitch knot. The other end of each rope should also be a taut line hitch.

7. Affix four small but strong twigs with miniature spikes into the ground at sufficient distances from the tarp's corners. Make sure the tarp will stretch after it's connected to the twigs. Ask an adult for help. If you can't find any twigs, you can use steel hooks.

8. Connect the open taut line hitches to the hooks, and your tarp shelter is ready!

Finding the Right Materials in Nature for Your Shelter

When looking for twigs, logs, branches, leaves, and pine needles, did you imagine yourself collecting them from live trees? That's a bad idea. It may snap while pulling down a low-hanging branch, and tiny, sharp wood pieces may pierce your skin. Chopping down trees for logs with an axe is highly unsafe for children. Furthermore, neither of these options is environmentally friendly. You should always respect nature, not harm it. So, how can you find the right materials to build your shelter?

The answer is simple. Look for dead trees or branches that have already fallen to the ground. In a forest, you may find quite a few of those. Is the bark of the trunk peeling off easily? Is its color white and unhealthy looking? Does it lack leaves on its branches? That's a dead tree for you.

Before carrying off the branches and logs, look for any sharp edges or spikes. Use a knife to prune the branch or ask an adult to do so. Dead branches and tree trunks are usually infested with pests and insects. Carry only those branches that have little to no infestation. It implies that the wood is strong enough to hold your shelter upright for a long time.

Dry leaves and fallen pine needles can be found in any wilderness region in the fall season. If it's not that time of the year yet, you can find a bunch in the arboretum section of the forest, a place where there is a nursery of plants. Alternatively, ask the forest officials where they store dry leaves after sweeping the forest floor.

If you find neither dry leaves nor pine needles, you can pluck dead grass from the vicinity of your camp. Only if you can't find anything else should you consider using live trees as the source of materials for your shelter. Make sure not to pluck anything from any rare or endangered species of plants and trees. Keep away from the poisonous plants. Avoid any plant or tree you cannot identify, or ask an adult for help.

Adapting Your Shelter for Different Weather Conditions

In the wilderness, the weather can change abruptly and dramatically. A light rain can transform into stormy winds. The leaves of your lean-to shelter probably won't stay put. Is the wind continuously lashing at your tarp from a fixed direction? Your tent may be leaning more to one side. Here are a couple of solutions to adapt to the changing weather conditions.

- **Build a Hut**

    A lean-to shelter is covered only on one side. The other side is wide open. What if the wind and rain change direction suddenly and come at you from the open side? Additionally, what if you want more privacy in your shelter? You don't have to build a specialized hut for this purpose. Just cover the other side, too!

    Collect more branches and leaves and let them lean on the open side. Make sure there is enough space from the direction of the main tree for you to crawl in. If not, remove a few branches and leaves from both sides on that end.

There is a small drawback to transforming your lean-to shelter into a hut. You cannot light a fire. You don't want to risk lighting it near the open end either because of the tree. You will have to decide what matters the most to you, your privacy or the comforting heat of a fire.

• Make a Lean-to Tarp

Just like you made a hut from a lean-to shelter, you can convert your tarp hut into a lean-to tarp. If the wind is especially fierce from one side, you can cover that side almost entirely with this transformation.

1. Unhook the two corners of one side of your tarp shelter (the one opposite the wind direction).
2. Tie the two corners to the main rope at either end. You can also tie them to the two trees with running bowline knots.
3. Pull out the hooks from the remaining two corners and pull them further back until the tarp is fully stretched.
4. Push the hooks back into the ground at those points.

Voila! Your lean-to tarp shelter is ready. It will be much more spacious than the tarp hut and better protect you from the one-sided wind or rain.

Section 5: Staying Safe from Wild Animals

Reading this chapter, you will learn how animals play a role in the world around you. You'll understand the importance of treating them with respect and giving them their space, and know how you can do it. This chapter also provides tips for how to hike safely and respect other people and wildlife while you're on the trail. Finally, you will know how to identify common types of wildlife and learn safety precautions.

Why Understanding and Respecting Wildlife Is Important

How do you behave when you're invited to someone's house? You probably avoid making a mess and being loud, right? You listen to and follow the house's rules, sit on chairs rather than countertops, and admire their decor and paintings without taking anything home. After dinner, you help with the dishes and clean up the toys before you leave.

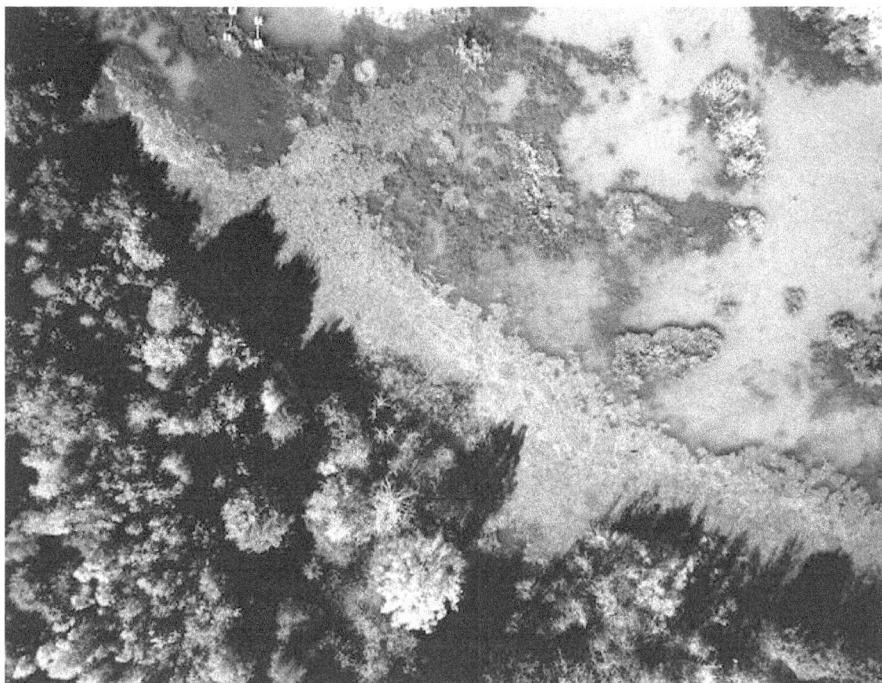

Protect the ecosystem by respecting its wildlife.

Visiting the wilderness is a lot like visiting someone's house. You become a guest in the homes of wildlife and must act as you would at someone else's house and how you expect others to act when they're at your place. In the wild, you should avoid making a mess and being so loud that you disturb animals and put yourself at risk. You should also sit on benches or other durable objects and clean up when you leave. You admire the animals and their habitat without taking anything home, even if it's just a shell or a log. If you do that, you may accidentally be taking away someone's home.

Maintaining the Ecosystem

Think of the ecosystem as a very large, strong team of nature and wildlife. Everything found in the wilderness has a special job to do. While each job may not seem big on its own, it affects several other wildlife species. If one piece of the ecosystem puzzle is missing, all other pieces are affected. Let's take plants, for example. Plants are necessary for survival because they provide food and oxygen. Plants need light from the sun to make food, and animals help spread plant seeds so more plants can grow. When leaves fall, bugs chew at them and help them break down. When leaves break down, they release nutrients into the soil, which new plants can absorb and grow strong and healthy.

Different wildlife species help each other maintain a balanced ecosystem. Bees, for example, pollinate plants so their seeds can spread and more of them can grow. In return for their hard work, plants give bees the nectar they need to make honey. Just like you have everything you need in the human world, wildlife has everything it needs in its ecosystem.

Respecting and Caring for Wildlife

Any interaction you have with wildlife, no matter how small it may seem, can affect its ecosystem and, therefore, harm it. Throwing a plastic bag into a pond, taking a shell home, or picking at plants negatively impacts the ecosystem's health and makes animals more aggressive.

Do you have a pet at home? If not, do you wish to have one? If you get a pet, you will care for it, feed it, and provide it with a safe and comfortable place to live. Wild animals are also living things that need similar things to survive. Earth is not just a human planet. You share it with pets, other animals in the wild, and all living things in nature. It's humans' responsibility to help these animals and avoid harming them and their homes. Therefore, you shouldn't litter or disturb wildlife. Animals have feelings, so you should avoid hurting them and try to help them when they're in trouble.

You should always watch animals from a distance when in the wild, even ones that seem cute and cuddly. You can use binoculars to get a closer look at them, but you should never approach them if you want to stay safe. You should also avoid feeding animals, no matter how hungry they may look. Human food is harmful to wildlife and doesn't contain the nutrients they need. Feeding wild animals regularly will also teach them to rely on you for food. They will no longer find their own meals, which would be a problem if no one else was there to feed them. Feeding animals also makes them less fearful of you, which can put you in danger or encourage them to follow you to unsafe areas, like roads, which can result in their injury.

Hiking Etiquette

Hiking is among the best ways to connect with nature. It is a fun activity that helps you relax and breathe clean, fresh air while exercising. The benefits of hiking are countless. However, you must know a few rules to make the most of your time.

- **Make Way for Climbers**: Climbing up the hill is a lot more work than climbing down. When you're descending, create enough space for those going uphill to pass through.

- **Meeting Bicyclists**: If you plan on cycling, check out the specific park or trail regulations to know whether it's allowed. Bicyclists should generally make way for hikers who are on foot, allowing them to pass first. If you're the one cycling, stop and step to the side whenever you see a hiker. Be mindful of plants and animals, and avoid accidentally hurting them with your bike or feet.

- **Gently Approach Horses:** Whether you're biking or on foot, you should give horses and other similar animals the right of way. Let them pass first. Keep in mind that these animals can get frightened easily, and any sudden movements can put them, those riding them, and even others in danger. Whenever you approach them, use a gentle voice to announce your presence.

- **Say Hello**: Be friendly to other people you encounter on the trail. Say "hello," and let them know you want to pass in a respectful way.

- **Don't Step Off the Trail**: Stay on the rail unless you must let someone else pass. Stepping on something you're not supposed to step on can damage the ecosystem, so be sure to mind where you're standing.

- **Don't Disturb Wildlife:** Use binoculars if you want to take a closer look at animals instead of stepping off the trail and putting them and yourself in danger.

- **Consider Weather Conditions:** Avoid hiking after it has just rained, as muddy and slippery trails are dangerous.

- **Minimize the Noise:** Loud noises on the trail can disturb wildlife and other hikers. Keep your phone on low volume and avoid engaging in loud conversations.

Common Types of Wildlife to Find in the Wilderness

A male deer is easy to identify because of its antlers.

- **Deer:** These animals are mostly found in forests and grassland. They vary in size depending on their species and age. Male deer are very easy to identify because they are characterized by their antlers, which grow as they age. Deer are generally active at sunrise and sunset. These animals eat plants and aren't considered dangerous to humans. However, they can display aggressive behavior if they feel threatened. It's best to keep your distance from them.

- **Raccoons:** Raccoons are small to medium-sized furry animals. They are usually grayish to brown in color and have patterns that mimic rings on their tails. They are most active at night and eat both meat and plants. They usually feed on plants, eggs, smaller animals, and insects. Raccoons generally don't attack humans, but they do if they feel threatened. They often carry harmful diseases, so you should keep your distance from them.

- **Skunks:** Skunks are small animals with black fur and white markings down their backs. They are popularly known for their ability to spray bad odors when they feel threatened. Like raccoons, skunks are mostly active at night and eat a wide array of foods. Avoid approaching or provoking skunks, as they might spray you or attack you when startled. Their spraying can be harmful, and the odor is difficult to get rid of.

- **Squirrels:** These small, furry animals come in a variety of colors, including gray, red, and brown. They are mostly active during the day and eat a varied diet, which includes insects, nuts, bird eggs, fruits, and seeds. Respect a squirrel's space and only watch them from a distance. While they are generally harmless, they may resort to biting if they feel scared.

- **Black Bears**: Black bears and brown bears are among the most popular of their species. While black bears grow to be very large, they are still smaller than brown bears. Black bears hibernate during winter and eat a varied diet that includes vegetables, nuts, berries, insects, and meat. You should keep a safe distance from bears at all times. Watch them from afar and make noises to make them aware of your presence.

- **Coyotes**: Coyotes are strong and intelligent medium-sized animals. They have grayish-brown fur and are mostly active during the night. They have a varied diet that ranges from fruit and vegetables to insects, birds, and small mammals. Don't approach coyotes at all, and avoid bringing your pets into areas where they are present. If you must bring a pet along, keep it on a leash beside you.

- **Birds:** Birds are among the most common wildlife you'll find in the wilderness. However, learning how to identify each bird species requires a guide or directory of its own. Each type of bird comes in its own shape, size, and color. Some bird types eat only seeds, some eat worms and other insects, and others eat a variety of both. Sparrows, Bluejays, and Robins are among the most commonly spotted birds. When observing birds, avoid approaching or disturbing them. Simply admire them or use an identification guide to learn more about them from afar.

Safety Precautions for Encountering Wild Animals

Bears

If you encounter a bear, you must communicate that you're a human. No matter how terrified you are, you should keep your voice calm while talking to it. This will allow the bear to identify that you aren't a prey animal. Stay still and wave your arms slowly. Don't be alarmed if the bear moves toward you or stands on its hind legs. This likely means that it's just curious and trying to better understand what you are.

Most bears don't want to attack you.

Remind yourself that most bears don't want to attack you. They may growl and engage in other defensive behaviors before they turn away and leave. Continue talking to the bear in a low, calm tone, and avoid screaming or making any sudden movements. You can move away slowly and sideways if the bear doesn't move.

Try not to break away from your group when you're out in the wild. Large groups can intimidate bears. Keep your food stored away, and don't try to escape by climbing up trees, as they'll probably follow you. Bear attacks are very rare, but it helps to be prepared. If you're attacked by a brown bear, play dead. If it's a black bear, try to escape or fight back. You should also keep bear pepper spray on you.

Coyotes

If a coyote approaches you, keep firmly clapping your hands. Alternate between clapping and swinging your hands all around you to make yourself appear larger than you really are. Through rocks, sticks, and other objects near it to scare it away from you. Keep a whistle or dog spray on you, and avoid running away. If the coyote keeps approaching you, slowly back away into somewhere you can hide.

Snake

If you see a snake, try to remain as calm as you can. The reptile is usually not aggressive unless you provoke it. Observe how it looks so you can identify it later and find out whether it's venomous. Calmly and slowly move away from it while watching it to ensure that it doesn't speed up.

All animals play a significant role in the maintenance of the ecosystem. When visiting wild animals in the wilderness, you must treat them with respect and give them the space they need to perform their daily activities. Otherwise, you'd be putting them and yourself in danger.

Section 6: Creating Useful Tools

Tools are the backbone of civilization. They are one of the main reasons humans are at the top of the food chain. They are used to cook, clean, build, break, make additional tools, and so much more. For your wilderness adventure, you may have already packed a few tools like a compass, a first aid kit, ropes, a topography map, a matchbox, a flashlight, etc.

Did you forget to carry a knife, though? What about a pickaxe or a hammer? How about weapons to defend yourself from possible predators? Even if you did manage to carry all these tools, your backpack must weigh a ton. Why overburden yourself when you can just create any required tool in the wilderness?

Simple Cutting Tools

A knife is a must to create tools out of materials found in nature. Did you forget to pack one? Don't worry. You can create your very own set of cutting tools! All you need is the right type of stone, a thread or a thin rope, and a small wooden stick.

Useful Stone Types

You can't just pick any rock from the ground and start shaping it to make a cutting tool. You will be using the cutting tool to make additional tools, so it should be hard enough and, at the same time, easily shaped into the desired form. Look for the following types of stones to create cutting tools.

- **Flint:** This type of rock is probably the easiest to recognize. It looks like wax but feels like glass. Its outer layer is thin, but it is quite hard inside, making it the perfect stone for molding into a cutting tool. To make sure the stone is indeed flint, strike it against a steel utensil and see if it produces sparks.

Flint is the easiest rock to recognize.

- **Obsidian:** This is one of the most commonly found rocks in the United States. It's a volcanic rock, so if you are headed to a place with a dormant or extinct volcano, you are bound to find it there. It looks like glass and is dark black in color.

Obsidian is a volcanic rock.

• **Jasper:** This has a similar appearance to obsidian, but it occurs in many different colors other than black. It's not as glassy-looking as obsidian.

Jasper occurs in many colors.
https://commons.wikimedia.org/wiki/File:Unpolished_jasper.jpg

• **Felsite:** This rock is defined by its different textures, and its colors can be a variety of black shades. It is also a volcanic rock, so if you cannot find obsidian, you can look for felsite.

Felsite is also a volcanic rock.
https://commons.wikimedia.org/wiki/File:Felsite_-orbicular_igneous_rock_Guanajuato_Mexico_2530.jpg

Other types of cutting stones include Rhyolite (found near felsite and obsidian) and Quartzite (usually found atop a hill).

How to Make Cutting Tools

Once you have found any of the above rocks, you need to shape them into a stone with sharp edges. If the stone is too big, start off by crushing it into smaller pieces. Pick another rock of the same size. Maintain a safe distance between yourself and the rock to be crushed (at least more than three feet). For added safety, put on biking glasses that cover your eyes entirely, along with riding gloves, thick shoes, a scarf, and full leather clothing.

Then, hurl the rock in your hand at the other rock with sufficient force. If your aim is true, both rocks will be smashed into each other and break apart into small pieces. You will find a readymade sharp-edged stone in the rubble if you are lucky. If not, pick a small piece (flat or elongated) and use the following techniques to create your cutting tool.

- **Percussion:** This technique is primarily shown in survival movies and TV shows. Take two stones, one harder than the other. Hold the softer stone in your palm and strike the hard stone at it with your other hand at an angle (a glancing motion). Tiny flakes from the softer stone will come off. Keep glance striking until a sharp point is produced. You can refine your cutting tool further by striking the other sides of the softer stone to make it into an arrowhead.

- **Bi-Polar Percussion:** This is a relatively safer way of creating a sharp-edged stone. Flakes and shards don't come off randomly here, but the motion is like striking a hammer on a nail, so you need to be very careful. Take a heavy stone with a flat face that can fit in your palm and another smaller, longer, and flatter stone that you want to make into a cutting tool. Hold the smaller stone upright with one hand (grip the middle) on a hard, flat surface, and ram the heavier stone with its flat surface on top of the smaller stone. The latter will be broken into two pieces, both having sharp edges. You can refine the pieces by using the regular percussion technique.

There are many other techniques, like pressure flaking and knapping, but they are much more complicated and are primarily used to refine your tools even further. Coarse tools made from basic percussion techniques are effective enough for now.

Making Cordage

Crafted a good, sharp cutting stone already? Great work! You can't hold it without a grip or a handle, however. Before you go looking for something to attach it to, find something to attach it with. A simple cotton or nylon thread would work. A thin rope would also do the trick. Did you forget to pack either of these things? You can make your very own fastening thread from natural fibers. It is called cordage.

You can use thin strips of bark to fasten your cutting stone to a handle, but there is a high chance that the strips may start thinning and break after heavy use. A cordage is much better and stronger. You will need dry strips of bark from a dead tree or dry strands of dead grass. In live trees, the strips are filled with moisture, so they won't make a strong cordage. Plus, peeling bark off a dead tree is eco-friendly, too.

Remove thin individual strands of fibers from the bark or grass. Follow these steps to make a simple cordage quickly.

1. Place a few individual strands on a flat surface.
2. Bring them together and hold their two ends with your fingers.
3. Roll the entire thing on the surface in a single direction. If you run out of the surface, bring it back and roll it again until the fibers are tightly wound.
4. Hold the middle of your makeshift cordage between your front teeth and stretch the two dangling ends downward with your fingers.
5. Let go of the middle and behold the cordage twisting around itself automatically!

Making a Grip

It is much easier to fashion a grip or a handle than a cordage or a cutting tool. Pick a moderately thick branch that is more or less straight. With your newly made cutting stone, shear the outer skin and cut off any sharp points. If you have sandpaper at hand, you can give a smooth finish to your handiwork.

Then, hold your cutting stone at the top edge of the newly-fashioned grip or handle. The sharp edge should be outward, and a small part of the lower edge should overlap with the grip's top edge. Hold this together with your finger as you wrap your cordage around the intersection. Make sure the wrapping is strong before tying up the loose ends. It mustn't come off after a few good strikes of the cutting tool to a hard surface.

Simple Primitive Weapons and Traps

Wildlife should be preserved, but it doesn't mean you should leave yourself defenseless. You will feel much safer with a spear in your hand and a bow slung on your shoulder. If you are hungry and have no edible plants nearby, a small game trap or a fishing spear will come in handy. You can't expect to use your makeshift simple cutting tool for all the work. (Show a picture of every type of weapon and trap below)

- Spear

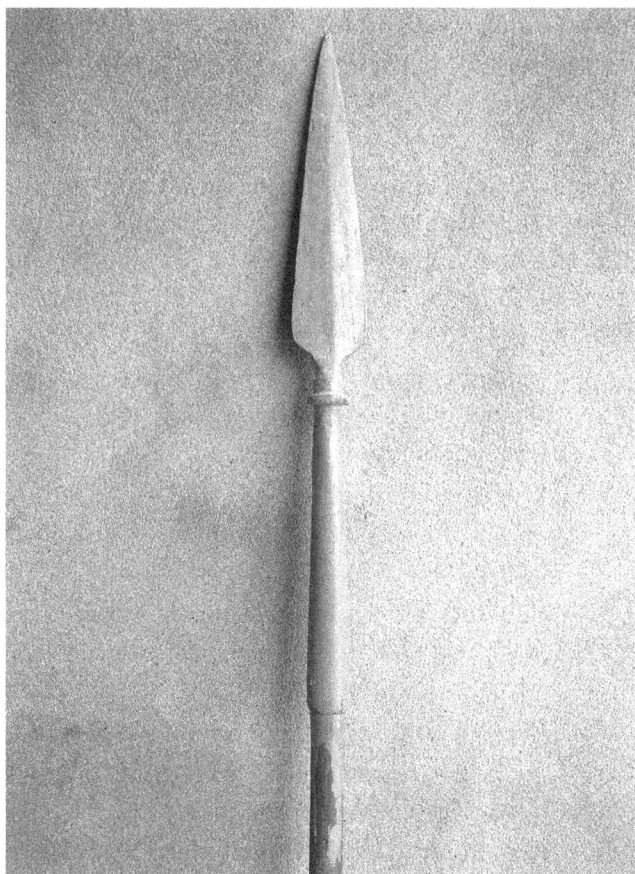

A spear is a longer version of a knife.

Gurnoor ghuman, CC BY-SA 4.0 <https://creativecommons.org/licenses/by-sa/4.0>, via Wikimedia Commons: https://commons.wikimedia.org/wiki/File:Spear_03.jpg

A spear is just a longer version of a knife. The Stone Age people used it to gain a bit of range while hunting. It can also be thrown like a javelin to attack a prey further off. Here's an easy and safe way to fashion a simple spear.

1. Find a long, straight branch from a dead tree (around six feet in length and an inch or two in diameter).

2. Remove the outer skin with your cutting tool, along with any sharp edges.

3. Hold it a few feet away from the edge in one hand, and with the cutting tool in the other hand, carve a sharp tip at the edge of the stick. It's just like sharpening your pencil with a knife.

Alternatively, you can affix an elongated and sharpened stone made from bipolar percussion to the stick with your cordage, the same way you created your cutting tool.

• Fishing Spear

Crafting a fishing spear is harder and more dangerous than a simple spear. Adult supervision is highly recommended. A fishing spear is a long stick with a claw-like opening used to skewer and trap the fish. You will need a thin, sharp knife to make this.

1. Find the same type of branch you did for the simple spear and clear the outer bark and sharp edges with your cutting tool or knife.

2. Use the side edge of the knife to bore through the top of the stick, splitting it in two for just around three to four inches.

3. Pull out the knife and split it again. This time, it is perpendicular to the first split. The structure will seem like four sticks attached to a pole.

4. Wrap a cordage at the base of the splits.

5. Push two small twigs between the splits perpendicular to each other. The twigs should be around half an inch in diameter. This is done to keep the claw open.

6. Tie another cordage around the stick and twigs.

7. Using your cutting tool or knife, sharpen each of the four edges of the claw, and your fishing spear is ready!

Once you learn how to work with the bones below, you can attach the sharpened bones to your spear to make it more effective.

• Fashioning Bone Tools

Bones are not only harder than stones but also flexible in nature. They are ideal for crafting hooks, spear points, and needles. They are also readily available in the wilderness from the decayed bodies of long-dead animals. When you find a bone, clean it first in a running stream of water. Alternatively, you can use the bones from the animal or fish you had for lunch.

The safest and easiest way to sharpen a bone is to smash it with a rock. There are bound to be a few sharp points among the debris. These shards are usually supple and can be bent to create a fish hook. Tie your cordage to the other end of the hook and fling it in a lake or a river to catch fish. You can use the harder, sharp-edged bones to replace the stones in your cutting tools and spears.

There are other ways of creating bone tools, like sawing and abrading, but they are highly advanced and unsafe for children.

• Small Game Trap

Want to catch animals without getting your hands dirty? The simplest small game trap you can create is a snare. Take your cord and tie a basic knot on one end, keeping an open wide loop. You can lasso the animal or set up a snare trap with the cord hanging from a tree branch. Keep some food near the loop. The animal's head will get stuck in the loop as it tries to pass through. The noose will tighten around its neck when it struggles to pull free. If catching wild animals is forbidden in the area, let the creature loose soon after.

Tool Maintenance and Repair

These makeshift tools created from stones and bones don't usually last long. You will need to sharpen and clean the tools after each use. If you'll be in the wilderness for a couple of days, create at least two cutting tools to maintain the edge of your other tools.

Does the cordage feel loose? Untie and refasten it. Is it fraying, and the thread is coming off? Replace it with fresh cordage. Has the stone point of your spear become small and blunt? Affix another sharp stone there. Make it a habit of maintaining and repairing your tools each morning and evening.

Section 7: First Aid and Emergencies

Whether venturing into the wilderness, embarking on a camping trip, hiking through rugged terrain, or simply enjoying a day at the beach, the great outdoors offers adventure and a connection to nature. However, it also presents inherent risks and challenges that can quickly turn a pleasant outing into an emergency. That's where the significance of first aid skills becomes evident.

With its unpredictable environments, wildlife encounters, and remote locations, the wilderness lacks immediate access to medical facilities and professional assistance. In these scenarios, your knowledge of first aid means the difference between a manageable incident and a life-threatening emergency.

Here are several key reasons why learning first aid skills is necessary for children, especially in the wilderness.

Rapid Response to Injuries

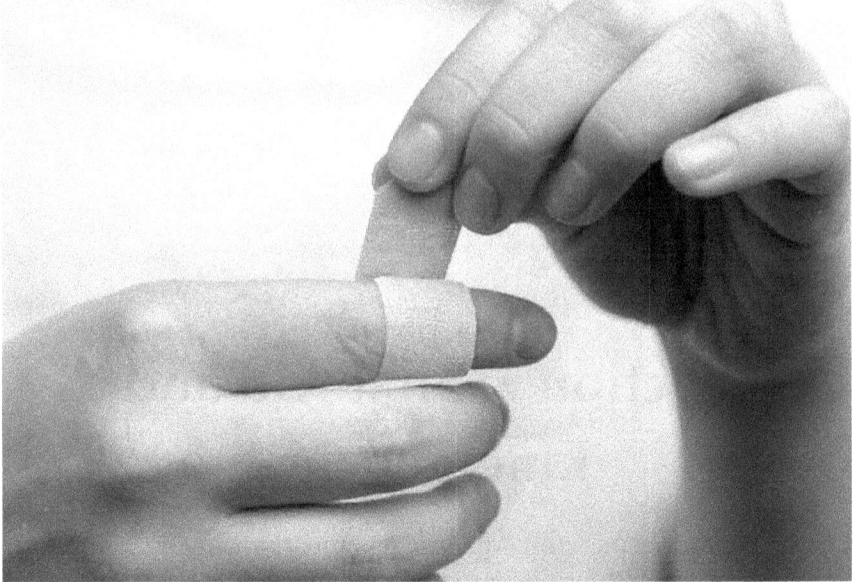

First aid knowledge can allow you to respond quickly.
https://unsplash.com/photos/person-with-band-aid-on-middle-finger-SwWjCbHoFE?utm_content=creditShareLink&utm_medium=referral&utm_source=unsplash

Accidents can happen in the blink of an eye – a fall, a burn, or a deep cut from a sharp object. First aid knowledge allows you to respond quickly, promptly addressing wounds, fractures, and other injuries, reducing the risk of complications and infections.

Saving Lives

In remote outdoor settings, it can take a long time for professional help to arrive. Learning first aid can save a life in dire situations, such as when someone is suffering from a heart attack, severe allergic reaction, or a near-drowning incident.

Alleviating Discomfort

Minor injuries like sprains, insect stings, and sunburns can disrupt an outdoor experience. First aid skills enable you to provide relief so you can continue your adventure rather than having to cut it short due to discomfort.

Enhancing Preparedness

Being well-prepared for outdoor activities means more than just packing the right gear. It's knowing how to use that gear and adapt to unexpected challenges. First aid skills provide you with the tools to stay calm, assess situations, and respond effectively, even in high-stress situations.

Encouraging Responsible Recreation

Having first aid knowledge promotes responsible outdoor recreation. It encourages individuals to respect the environment, leave no trace, and be more considerate of their fellow outdoor enthusiasts, contributing to the overall well-being of natural spaces.

Whether you've been on many outdoor adventures or are just starting to explore nature, these skills are essential.

Basic Wilderness First Aid Kit

Assembling a basic wilderness first aid kit is crucial for outdoor activities, as it ensures that you have the necessary supplies to address common injuries and emergencies while keeping the kit compact and portable. Begin with a durable, waterproof container to store your first aid supplies. Options include zip-lock bags, small waterproof pouches, or dedicated first-aid kits available in outdoor stores.

List of Items to Include

- **Sterile Gauze Pads:** These are used for cleaning and covering wounds.
- **Adhesive Bandages**: Use them to protect small cuts and blisters.
- **Adhesive Tape**: Helps secure dressings and immobilize injured areas.
- **Antiseptic Wipes or Solutions:** These are crucial for cleaning wounds and preventing infection.
- **Tweezers:** Handy for removing splinters or debris from wounds.
- **Pain Relievers (e.g., Acetaminophen or Ibuprofen):** Helpful for minor aches and pains.
- **Antihistamines (e.g., Benadryl):** Useful for treating allergic reactions to insect stings, food, or plants.
- **Sunscreen**: Protect your skin from harmful UV rays, especially on sunny days. You can also add a lip balm to prevent chapped lips and sunburn.
- **Insect Repellent:** Keeps mosquitoes and other bugs away.

- **Skin Protection:** Calamine lotion or hydrocortisone cream: Treat skin irritations and bug bites.
- **Wound Care Bandages**: Steri-strips or butterfly bandages: Use for closing small wounds.
- **Scissors**: Small scissors or a multi-tool with scissors: Handy for cutting tape and clothing.
- **Whistle**: Use to signal for help in an emergency.
- **Documentation:** A copy of your personal identification, medical history, and any relevant contact numbers. This information is vital for medical professionals in case of severe emergencies.
- **Manual:** A basic first aid manual of instructions for common wilderness injuries.
- **Personal Supplies**: Any personal items specific to your needs, such as extra prescription medications, medical bracelets, or other condition-specific supplies.

After completing the items checklist, review the contents again and ensure your first aid kit is compact, lightweight, and easily accessible. Avoid filling the kit with too many disposable items or medications, as it will only make your kit heavier. For example, you may need a few tablets for each medication instead of carrying the entire pack. Likewise, a pair or two of gloves will suffice instead of packing a dozen in your first-aid kit.

You should be able to attach it to your backpack or belt using carabiners or straps or keep it in an outer pocket. Make sure everyone in your group knows where the kit is and how to use its contents. Regularly inspect your first aid kit, replacing damaged, expired, or used items. Having the supplies is not enough; you must learn how to use them correctly.

Evaluating the Severity of Injury

Assessing the severity of injuries and prioritizing care, especially for life-threatening injuries, is a critical skill when faced with an emergency outdoors. You must stay calm and assess the situation to provide effective and timely first aid. Here's a step-by-step guide on how to do this:

Maintain Your Composure

First and foremost, stay calm. Panic affects your ability to provide appropriate care. Take a few deep breaths to help you focus.

Ensure Your Safety

Before rushing to help others, evaluate the scene for potential hazards, such as falling rocks, unstable terrain, or dangerous wildlife. Move to a safe location if necessary.

Call for Help

If you have access to communication (cell phone or radio), call for emergency assistance immediately. In remote areas, a satellite communication device is a lifesaver.

Assess Responsiveness

Gently tap or shake the injured person and ask if they are okay. Determine their level of consciousness and responsiveness.

Check for Breathing

If the person is unresponsive, check for breathing. Place your ear near their mouth and nose while looking at their chest for any rise and fall. If they are not breathing or are breathing abnormally, begin CPR if you are trained to do so.

Survey for Life-Threatening Bleeding

Look for life-threatening bleeding, which can be arterial and lead to severe blood loss. Apply pressure to the wound with a sterile bandage (if available) or any clean cloth. If the bleeding is profuse and doesn't stop, consider applying a tourniquet above the wound if you know how to do this correctly.

Assess for Shock

Check for signs of shock, which can occur with severe injuries. Symptoms include rapid, shallow breathing, confusion, paleness, and cold, clammy skin. If shock is suspected, keep the injured person warm, elevate their legs slightly, and reassure them.

Airway Management

If the person is conscious but has difficulty breathing due to an obstruction, perform first aid measures to clear the airway. This could include the Heimlich maneuver for choking. (If you don't know how to perform this maneuver, ask an adult to show you!)

Continue Assessment

Assess the injured person for other injuries or medical conditions. Prioritize care based on the severity of these issues. For example, a head injury, a compromised airway, or a spinal injury should be addressed as soon as a priority over less severe injuries. Continue to monitor the injured person's condition and adjust your care as needed. Remember, conditions can change, so regularly check on the injured person.

Comfort and Reassure

Throughout the process, provide emotional support and reassurance to the injured person. Keeping them calm can have a positive impact on their recovery.

Remember that staying calm and organized in your approach is essential in any emergency. Assess the situation, identify life-threatening injuries, and provide immediate care as needed while waiting for professional help to arrive. Your ability to prioritize and provide care can make a significant difference in the outcome of an emergency in the wilderness.

Treating Minor Wounds

1. Ensure the area is safe and free from hazards.
2. Wash your hands or use hand sanitizer if water is unavailable.
3. Examine the wound for its size, depth, and cleanliness. If it's a minor cut or scrape, proceed.
4. Clean the wound.
5. Rinse the wound gently with clean water to remove dirt and debris.
6. If available, use an antiseptic wipe or solution to clean the wound.
7. Pat the area dry with a clean cloth or sterile gauze.
8. Apply an Antibiotic Ointment: If you have antibiotic ointment, apply a thin layer to prevent infection.
9. Place a sterile adhesive bandage or dressing over the wound.
10. Change the bandage daily and keep the wound clean.
11. Over-the-counter pain relievers can help manage discomfort.

Treating Strains

1. Encourage the individual to rest and avoid using the injured area.

2. Apply an ice pack wrapped in a cloth to reduce swelling and pain. However, if you have trouble finding ice in your surroundings, use water from a nearby stream or lake, dip a clean cloth in it, and compress the injured area.

3. Use an elastic bandage to provide support.

4. Elevate the injured area above heart level to minimize swelling.

Over-the-counter pain relievers can help manage pain and inflammation—allow time for the strain to heal. Seek medical attention if the pain or swelling worsens or doesn't improve.

Treating Burns

1. Ensure there is no ongoing risk of burn (e.g., remove the person from the heat source).

2. Run cold water over the burn for about 10-20 minutes or until the pain subsides.

3. If there are blisters, leave them intact to prevent infection.

4. If available, apply an over-the-counter burn ointment.

5. Use a sterile, non-stick dressing or a clean cloth to cover the burn.

First Aid for Snakebites

1. Panic can worsen the situation. Encourage the person to keep the bitten limb as still as possible.

2. Remove any tight clothing, jewelry, or accessories near the bite site that could constrict blood flow if swelling occurs.

3. If possible, keep the affected limb slightly elevated to reduce swelling.

4. Call for emergency help and get to the nearest medical facility as soon as possible.

5. Note the time of the bite.

First Aid for Stings

1. If a stinger is present (as in bee or wasp stings), gently scrape it off with a flat-edged object like a credit card.

2. Clean the sting site with soap and water.

3. Use a cold pack to reduce pain and swelling.

Infection Prevention

4. Wash wounds regularly with soap and water.
5. Keep dressings clean and dry. Change them daily.
6. Picking at scabs can increase the risk of infection.
7. Watch for redness, increasing pain, pus, or fever. Seek medical attention if these signs appear.

Seeking Medical Attention

In case of burns or strains, try seeking immediate medical attention. For snake bites, even a non-venomous snake, seek medical attention for wound care and tetanus prevention. For allergic reactions, if the injured person shows signs of a severe allergic reaction, such as difficulty breathing or swelling of the face, lips, or tongue, call 911 or emergency services.

In all cases, if there's any doubt or concern about the severity of the injury, it's best to seek professional medical help. Prompt medical attention can prevent complications and ensure the best possible outcome for the injured person.

Using Whistles and Signaling Devices

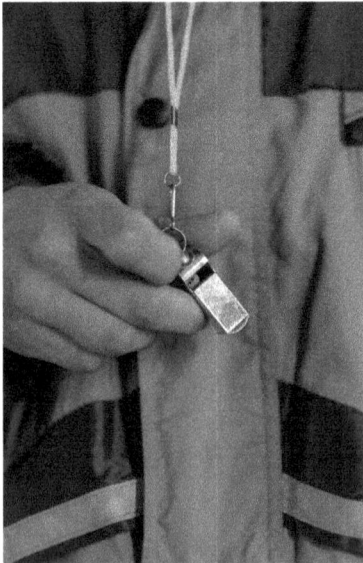

A whistle can help you call for help.
https://www.pexels.com/photo/hand-holding-a-whistle-7207354/

- Make sure you carry a whistle when you're out in the wilderness. Whistles are like your superpower for calling for help.
- Learn this special whistle code: three quick, short blasts, then pause and do it again. It's the secret signal to tell others you need help.
- If you need to use your whistle, find a place with lots of room where people can see and hear you. It's easier for your signal to travel in wide-open areas.
- When you blow your whistle, do it with enough force so the sound travels far, but don't exhaust yourself. A short, strong blow is perfect.
- If you're in trouble, blow your whistle three times, pause, and do it again. Keep doing this until help arrives or someone answers.
- Besides whistles, you can also use signal mirrors, flashlights, or anything colorful that stands out. Make sure you know how to use them, too.

When to Signal for Help

- Suppose something really scary happens, like a bad injury, getting lost, or coming across a dangerous animal. In that case, it's time to use your whistle.
- If you're too tired or something else makes it impossible to continue what you were doing, blow your whistle for help.
- If you're not prepared for the weather conditions, like a storm or extreme heat, use your whistle to call for help.

Seeking Adult Help for Serious Emergencies

- Remember, while you're learning cool first aid and survival skills, the real heroes are the grown-ups. If something *really bad* happens, don't be shy – get an adult right away.
- If you have a phone or a radio, use it to talk to the grown-ups in your group. Tell them what's happening, and they'll know what to do. They can call for professional help, like park rangers or doctors.
- Make sure you know important numbers, like 911. That's the fastest way to reach the right grown-ups when things get tough.

By using your whistle and other signaling devices wisely and calling in the grown-ups when there's a big emergency, you'll be all set for safe and fun outdoor adventures.

Section 8: Finding Your Way

In this chapter, you will learn navigational skills to help you explore the wilderness and find your way back to safety in emergencies. This chapter explains what cardinal directions are and why they're useful. It also teaches you how to read a map and use natural cues like the sun, stars, and shadows to find directions. You'll also find tips on marking trails and paths to trace your way back to safety or help rescuers find you in case of emergencies.

What Are Cardinal Directions?

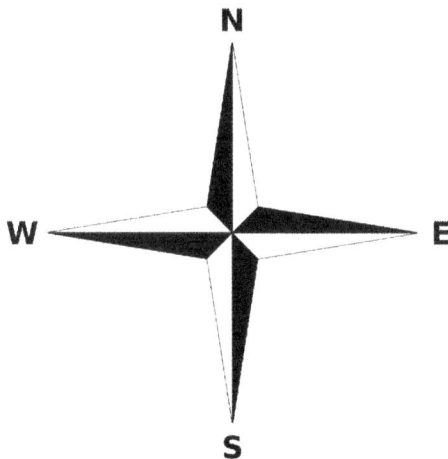

The cardinal directions.

Directions are methods of communication that help people explain and understand what things are in relation to others. An example of giving directions would be saying that the coffee shop is on the left side of the restaurant. However, this can be very confusing if you aren't facing the restaurant. This is where cardinal directions come in.

Cardinal directions give accurate geographic directions as they don't depend on the direction you're facing. North, South, East, and West are the main cardinal directions in geography. If you're facing a map, the north will refer to the upper part of the map, the south will refer to the lower one, the west will refer to where your left hand is holding the map, and the east will be where your right hand is.

For instance, if someone says, "The coffee shop is found west of the restaurant," you won't have to face a certain way to get there correctly. West will always be west regardless of where you're standing. If you know which states are on the map, you can easily tell which part of the USA you're in and which direction you need to go to get to another state.

For instance, if you want to travel from Wyoming, which is in North America, to New Mexico, you would have to travel south. If you want to go from California, which is located in the west, to Utah, you would have to travel east. You can use a compass or a map to know where you're located and which direction you need to head in. You can also use natural cues like the sun and the stars to know where to go.

How to Read a Map

Maps are considered one of the easiest ways to navigate.
https://pixabay.com/photos/passport-map-world-trip-tourism-2714675/

Maps are considered one of the easiest ways to navigate and understand geographical information. A map gives you a bird's view of the area and presents all the necessary information.

Step 1: Read the Title

Reading the map's title is the first and most important step in reading a map. There are many different types of maps. There are maps of the Earth, which tell you where each country is located. There is a map for each country, which includes the location of every city and other geographic features like mountains, deserts, forests, and rivers. There are maps of each city and even town that tell you how to get to certain shops, malls, parks, restaurants, and so on.

Some maps illustrate significant routes in history, such as a map of the Silk Road, one of the most important trade routes. It shows the key locations of the trade route, where it started and connected to, various branches of the routes, and how traders could choose between different paths. There are also maps illustrating the migration patterns of certain animals at different times of the year.

Reading the title helps you determine if this is the map you need. If you're in Milan, Italy, a map of a different city, such as Firenze, wouldn't help. You should also pay attention to the date on which the map was created. You should use recent maps to ensure that they're up to date. You don't want to use a map to get to a restaurant only to discover that this map was created in 1958 and that a hair salon has taken its place.

Step 2: Know Its Orientation

To use a map correctly, you should know where each cardinal direction lies on the map. You don't want to hold it upside down accidentally. Fortunately, most maps have a small illustration of a compass that is labeled N (north), S (south), E (east), and W (west), allowing you to orient the map correctly.

Step 3: Know Its Scale

Maps are accurate yet scaled-down representations of certain areas and movements. A map that is true to size would be very impractical. A map is similar to what it would look like if you took a very high-quality picture of an entire country and printed it onto paper. The picture would show the exact location of everything in the country, but in a much smaller size than it really is. Knowing the scale of the map means knowing the real distance between locations. When using a map to navigate, this is the only way you'll know how far you need to travel to get to your target area.

Step 4: Use the Map's Key

Most maps have a key or a legend that tells you what different illustrations on the map mean. Map makers use different shapes, symbols, colors, and forms of lines and arrows to communicate different things. For instance, a blue square could mean a lake, a blue line could mean a river, a tree may refer to a park, and a dashed line could represent mountains.

Remember that there isn't one key or legend that all maps stick to. Therefore, you should refer to the specific legend offered on the map you're using.

Step 5: Determine the Borders

After you've learned the basics of reading a map, you need to determine where the place you're searching for is in real life. To do that, you need to understand that some maps use a standard grid pattern, which means that it's divided into many small equal squares based on the latitude and longitude. The latitude is an imaginary line that runs vertically down the Earth, from the North Pole to the South Pole, while the longitude is an imaginary line that runs across the Earth vertically. It is located halfway between the North and South Poles.

The longitude and latitude help with navigation and mapping. Even today's GPS apps and devices use longitude and latitude to function correctly. They are also used to identify locations on the map and help with weather forecasting.

The grid can either be visible or invisible on the map. Dividing the map into squares helps you determine exactly where places lie. Other maps, especially if they represent smaller areas, such as cities, may use their own system or code consisting of numbers and letters. This code helps map readers find places in real life. The code usually tells you which line to follow up and down, according to the longitude, and which line to follow side to side, according to the latitude.

Finding Directions Using the Sun and the Stars

Finding Directions in the Morning

The sun helps you locate the north, which can help you find all the other directions. You'll only need a relatively straight stick that is around 1 meter long.

1. Find a place that is bush-free and push the stick into the ground. It's okay if the stick leans a little. The most important

thing is that you're able to see a clear shadow of it on the ground.

2. Use a stone or any small tool to mark the stick's shadow on the ground.

3. Wait for 10 to 15 minutes until the stick's shadow has moved, and use another tool to mark the new shadow.

4. Use your finger or another stick to draw a straight line, connecting the first and second rocks or markings together. Continue drawing the line about a foot past the second marking.

5. Stand facing the shadows, with your left toe at the first marking and your right toe at the end of the line you just drew. You are now facing the true north.

6. You can easily find the other directions now that you're facing north.

7. Draw a line across the line you drew, creating a cross. Mark the directions on it.

Finding Directions at Night

If you're in the northern hemisphere, these instructions will help you.

The Big Dipper can help you find the North Star.

The Big Dipper is a group or constellation of seven stars that can help you determine where the North Star is. The Big Dipper looks like a line connecting to the bowl. The two stars at the end of the bowl are called pointers. You will find the North Star if you trace a straight line out from the pointers. The Big Dipper slowly rotates around the North Star, constantly changing its location. However, if you trace a straight line from the pointers, it'll lead to the North Star.

You can also use Cassiopeia, a constellation of five stars, to locate the North Star. This constellation resembles the letter "M" a little. Draw an imaginary line down the letter, extending it from the part where it opens. The straight line should connect to the North Star.

If you're in the southern hemisphere

Find the Southern Cross, a constellation of four stars that looks like a tilted cross, to determine the direction of the south. The two stars that create the longer line in the cross are called pointers. Extend a line from the end of the cross (around five times longer than its length). From this point, draw a line downward and choose a landmark, such as a mountain range, to mark the direction of the south.

Use Trail Markers

Marking the trail as you go along helps you avoid getting lost. You can always trace your steps back by following your markings. Trail markers are also important for your safety because they help rescuers find you in an emergency.

- Most people use chalk to mark key locations on the journey. You can use symbols that mean different things or write short messages for yourself. Chalk is one of the best ways to mark your trail without harming the environment, as it usually washes off after a couple of days.

- Chalk might not be suitable if the weather is damp or rainy. In this case, you should consider using environmental materials like rock cairns, stones, sticks, and pine cones. You can also paint marks on trees or place ribbons, but these options may not be suitable if you're walking along private property or in national parks.

Now you know the basics of navigation and wayfinding. You know how to read a map, a skill most people don't know how to do! You can navigate your way around cities without relying on GPS and can determine the cardinal directions by using only the sun and the stars. Besides being valuable knowledge, this is very cool information to have!

Section 9: Additional Survival Hacks

In this section, you will find several tips, hacks, and advice on enhancing your wilderness and survival skills. With this additional knowledge, you will thrive in the great outdoors. You will learn how to mentally, physically, and emotionally deal with emergencies and safely observe the wildlife. You will also learn about a few multi-purpose household tools you should consider packing.

Emergency Signaling

Learning how to signal for emergencies is among the most vital survival skills. Things can go wrong even when you least expect them to. You might lose your group, find yourself in severe weather conditions that are difficult to navigate through, get injured, fall ill, or become extremely exhausted and dehydrated. Being in the wild, where there isn't any mobile signal or internet, requires you to learn other methods to ask others for help.

S.O.S.

S.O.S. stands for "save our souls" or "save our ship." It is the most popular signal, as people worldwide understand it's a call for help. Morse code S.O.S. is a pattern consisting of three dots, three dashes, and three dots "...---...". The Morse code was used to communicate important messages through electric currents during World War 2.

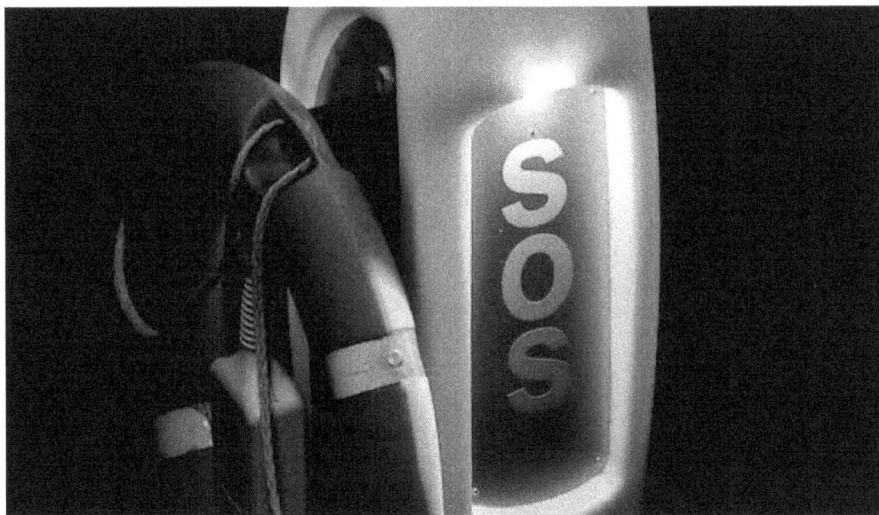

S.O.S. stands for "Save Our Souls."

This signal can be done through either sound or light. You can use a pipe or any other strong material and bang it on a hard surface to do this code "...---..." in the form of sound. Ask your parents to help you look up what the S.O.S. Morse Code sounds like and the right way to do it. Learn and practice it in case you ever need to do it.

Using a flashlight is another way to use the S.O.S. Morse Code. To do it, you'll turn your flashlight on and off quickly three times, then turn it on and hold for a few seconds before turning it back off three times, and then turn it on and off quickly three more times. You can also look up how to do the S.O.S. signal using a flashlight on YouTube. This method, of course, works best at night. You can direct your flashlight at a passing airplane.

If you have a hunter in your group, ask them to fire three shots in the air to signal the need for help. If you have a car, you can honk and flash the headlights in patterns of three. Packing two-way radios and agreeing on a certain frequency to communicate on is a great idea. This way, lost individuals can press the transmit button in patterns of three to signal distress. However, always have a backup plan as these radios only work within a certain range of communication.

Reflected Sunlight

If you need to call for help in the morning, use a mirror to reflect sunlight. You can buy specialized mirrors at a camping store or use any reflective surface. Use your fingers to create a "V" or peace sign at the target you want help from. Keep moving the mirror with your other hand until you find the position that allows the reflection of the sunlight to face the target. Do this in patterns of three to show that you need help. You should never flash signals at airplanes unless you are in an actual emergency.

Build a Fire

After finding water, food, and shelter, learning to build a fire is the most important survival skill. You need fire to stay warm when the temperature drops, scare off some potentially dangerous wild animals, and, of course, have a source of light. If an emergency happens during the day, you can put grass, rubber tires, or green vegetation on your fire to make more smoke without putting it out. Be careful not to let the fire get out of control. At night, create three fires that take the shape of a triangle. Avoid building the fire among the trees or in a hidden area so people can see it clearly.

Use Bright Colors

Use any brightly-colored item that doesn't blend in with the environment to attract people's attention. Use clothes, blankets, sleeping bags, and any other materials to spell out large words like "S.O.S." or "HELP" on the ground. Each letter should be around 12 feet long. If you don't have that many items to use, you can stomp the words into the snow or use a stick to dig the words into the sand. You can even arrange rocks to spell the words out on the ground. Make sure, however, to put some colored items into trees around the area so your call for help can be seen. You can also create a flag with a red cloth attached to the end of the longest stick you can find and wave it to any plane or other passersby.

Glowing Light Stick

Swinging a glowing light stick to create the shape of a circle can grab the attention of potential helpers. Put a string through one end of a chemical light stick and swing it around to create a huge luminant circle. Keep in mind that these sticks can only be lit up once, but they usually last for around 8 to 12 hours.

Observing Wildlife

Nothing is worse than going on a trip in the wild, expecting to see many amazing creatures, but leaving without seeing any! You need to do some things to ensure a successful wildlife observation trip without putting yourself or the animals in danger.

Consider the Location and Time

To avoid disappointment, don't expect to see animals that aren't where you'll be. Research which animals live in the area you'll be visiting. Find out what they look like, learn about their behaviors, read about safety concerns regarding the animal, and know when they're most active. Also, consider the time of year you'll be visiting, as some animals hibernate during winter.

Start Exploring Early

Most animals are active either early in the morning or in the evening. Wake up early to start exploring and observe animals in the daylight. You may not find many animals in the afternoon when it's generally sunny and dry.

Stay Quiet and Attentive

Animals can sense your presence before you even realize you're there. In most cases, they'll flee to protect themselves, and you won't get to see them. So, be very quiet when observing in the wild, keep your cell phone on silent, and avoid talking to others. Be careful not to step on twigs or leaves or bump into anything to avoid making noise. Listen attentively to any movements in your surroundings to easily spot animals and determine their presence.

Consider the Wind and Smell

Most animals have a very sharp sense of smell. They can pick up on even the slightest odors from miles away. Believe it or not, some animals' sense of smell is much stronger than their eyesight! They will likely smell you before they can see you, so avoid spraying perfume on, applying scented body lotions, or using and carrying other scented items. Try to move against the direction of the wind so your scent doesn't get carried over.

Blend In

Blend in with the surrounding environment and avoid wearing bright colors. If you're in the forest, wear earthy tones like brown and green. If it's snowy, dress in white or light colors.

Find a Good Spot and Wait

Find a good spot and wait from a distance. Waiting for animals to pass by can feel extremely boring. However, remember that you'll see more animals if you wait and stay still rather than actively searching for wildlife.

Survival Psychology

Survival psychology refers to the mental and emotional attitudes you need to survive challenging situations in the wilderness. Practicing survival psychology helps you keep calm and focus when things get tough, allowing you to make quick and smart decisions. It is key to managing your fear and staying composed to do the right thing.

For instance, if you see a bear, it is generally recommended that you stay still and quiet. However, someone who goes into panic mode might end up screaming and running, which may trigger an attack. If you get lost, do your best to stay calm so you can create emergency signals with the resources you have. On the other hand, someone who feels panicked won't be able to think clearly and come up with practical solutions.

Start by taking a few deep breaths when you're in a challenging situation. This helps put your mind at ease and decrease worry. Breathe in slowly on 4 counts, hold your breath for 4 counts, and breathe out on 4 counts. Breathe normally for another 4 counts, and repeat until you feel calmer. Maintaining a positive mindset is also crucial when you're in trouble. You have to remind yourself that rescue and survival are possible.

If you're lost, think about everything you need to do to survive, such as finding shelter, food, and water. Tackle the list of things in order of most to least important. Remember that resting and taking a half-hour break when you feel exhausted before resuming your plan is fine.

Additional Survival Tools

The following are some household tools that can help you survive in the wilderness:

Large, Durable Garbage Bags

Large, durable, high-quality garbage bags can be used to store items safely or even create a shelter in times of emergencies. You can use heavy-duty garbage bags to make clothing articles, waterproof beds, or raincoats. You can also use garbage bags to collect or store water when you're running out.

Hand Sanitizer

If you're out in the wild, you probably have limited to no access to water and soap. Using hand sanitizer regularly will help you stay clean and hygienic and avoid illnesses and diseases.

Duct Tape

Duct tape can help secure your shelter, make it waterproof, repair broken items, and patch up ruined clothes.

Chapstick

Even though Chapstick is mainly used for cosmetic purposes, this tool is indispensable in the wilderness. Chapstick can stop wounds from bleeding, ease sunburn, and even serve as candles.

Aluminum Foil

Foil can be used in many ways.

You can use aluminum foil to collect water, create plates and bowls, and even make frying pans. This material is also useful for emergency signaling, as it's highly reflective. You can start fires using aluminum foil and AA batteries, as well.

Now you know what to do in case of emergencies when you're out in the wilderness. You should be able to devise a solid plan of action if you get lost or injured and know which items to pack to make life easier out in the wild.

Thank You Message

"May your trails be crooked, winding, lonesome, dangerous, leading to the most amazing view. May your mountains rise into and above the clouds."

Edward Abbey

Taking an interest in a new skill and investing time to read and learn about it is an admirable habit. You should be proud of yourself for coming this far. While the main point of spending time in the wild is stepping out of your comfort zone, connecting with nature, and doing all sorts of exciting and fun activities, you have to remain mindful of your surroundings. The priority is to stay safe and sound while still enjoying yourself.

Your journey doesn't end with these pages, as there are so many more tips and tricks you can explore to enhance and add to your camping experience.

As important as it is to learn what to do in certain situations, you must remember that practice makes perfect, and words are not a substitute for trial and expertise.

Camping is a magical experience that builds character and allows you to explore parts of yourself you didn't know existed. Nature is a good teacher regarding resilience, endurance, and patience. Remember that it's also a great opportunity to bond and forge stronger connections with the people you care about through common experiences and lasting memories.

The skills you'll learn from your exposure to the wilderness will not only serve you in the outdoors. The more you learn how to depend on yourself and survive in challenging circumstances, the more confidence you'll gain. You'll find that your self-worth rises and is reflected in every other aspect of your life. You'll see noticeable positive changes in your physical and mental health.

The best way to learn about the wilderness is by trying, jumping right into the fire, and foraging for yourself on the narrow terrains of the forest.

As you delve more into the natural world, you'll feel more at home and more in sync with Mother Nature. No homework, no exams, no stress, just you and the open green road, free to be yourself without any judgment.

Part 2: Knot Tying for Kids

A Fun and Easy Guide to Mastering Essential Knots for Young Adventurers

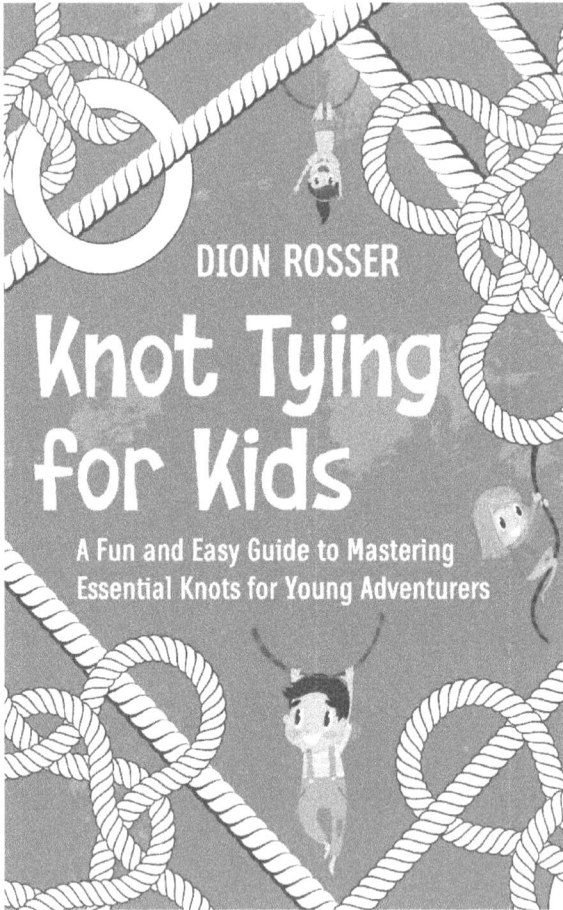

DION ROSSER

Knot Tying for Kids

A Fun and Easy Guide to Mastering Essential Knots for Young Adventurers

Introduction Letter to Parents

Dear Parents,

Every parent's and guardian's dream is to see their children grow up to become independent and self-sufficient adults. For this to happen, children must learn numerous essential skills that will help them navigate through the complexities of life. Knot tying is fun – but also a handy skill that teaches children problem solving, memorization, and critical thinking.

While mastering knot tying is often recommended for outdoor adventurers, your child can benefit from it even if they aren't interested in exploring the wilderness. They can incorporate this skill into a fun hobby or simply use it to navigate everyday life more efficiently. They can save themselves a lot of time and trouble by mastering basic everyday knots (like shoe laces), advanced knots if they wish to help with the boat, and various creative projects to pass the time – without a screen! This book has all the tools to help them do that.

Knot tying is challenging; some children will take more time to learn it, but this book will ensure they'll get there. Don't worry if your child didn't acquire this or similar skills through traditional means before; perhaps they just had trouble paying attention to intricate or tedious instructions. With easy-to-follow practical steps, this book is designed to guide young learners through the knot-tying process regardless of their abilities or experience level.

Help your child get started learning knot-tying safely and responsibly. There are some safety rules in the beginning chapters, providing a head start in helping you be the supportive parent your child needs as they embark on their knot-tying journey.

Have fun!

Introduction Letter to Children

Hey there!

Did you know that knot-tying has been used for centuries – and not just for securing things. While tying a secure knot does come in handy in everyday situations, like preventing your shoelaces from becoming untied, knots can also have many other purposes. From ceremonial functions to art to hunting and fishing, knot tying has played a central part in the lives of different cultures and civilizations since ancient times. If you love exploring the great outdoors, you'll find this skill particularly handy as it can help you remain safe and resolve any issues that might come up during your adventures.

Knot tying can also be a fun activity you might enjoy during your free time. Plenty of arts and crafts require knots for completing or creating projects. You can use knots to express whatever you feel or think, just like you would use drawing, coloring, or any other art form. Not only that, you'll learn other skills along the way, like being resourceful in tricky situations and solving seemingly insurmountable problems.

Whatever draws you to knot tying, you're about to find the gateway to exciting discoveries in the world of knots and your own abilities. Mastering this skill will teach you much about yourself, including your likes and dislikes and strengths and weaknesses. It will also help you work on those strengths or weaknesses and be more confident in navigating the world around you. You'll learn patience and the value of hard work, but FUN work!

If you're ready to embark on this exciting journey into the world of knot-tying, you can start by reading the first chapter!

Section 1: Knots in History

When you think of knots, you probably think of tying your shoelaces or knots sailors use on boats. While these might be the most universal uses for knot tying, the art has been around for thousands of years, and knots have been used for many other purposes throughout the centuries. Knots, created by tying a piece of string, cord, or rope, have evolved from simple fastenings for everyday objects to complex structures for arts and crafts projects.

Often, finding a new purpose for a knot tie led to the discovery of new uses for universal objects or the invention of other objects. Nowadays, you can tie a knot virtually in infinite ways, depending on what you'll be using it for. By reading this section, you'll learn how knot tying was featured across history and how important this skill was in different cultures.

Knot tying is an art that has been around for thousands of years.
https://pixabay.com/photos/flower-lis-knot-darling-rope-1934110/

An Ancient Tool

The earliest evidence of people using knots coincides with the use of primitive tools. We believe humans have used ropes for at least 15,000–17,000 years; this is an estimate – historians think the use of ropes could possibly even predate the invention of fire! Other tools, like the axe and wheels, were invented much later, and rope tying played a crucial role in their creation. The first axes were simple stone heads tied to wood handles.

Somewhere between 8,000 and 6,500 BC, people began to create textile fabrics for clothes and other purposes. They tied and secured the different pieces of material with knots. As the civilizations developed further, so did the use of knots and rope to create other devices and structures. Some of the first mechanisms knots were used for were fishing and hunting traps.

Around 4,000 BC, the Egyptians invented a *spindle*, which made creating ropes much easier. By the third century BC, Roman warriors went into battle armed with sling bolts they made from ropes tied into knots.

Jumping a little farther ahead in history to 1,200 AD, the Arab nations were creating knots to secure their garments and household textiles and decorate them. As sea travel picked up, so did the import of this knot-tying art. Soon, the Europeans were using it to adorn their clothes.

By this time in history, knot tying grew from creating simple knots (like the *overhand knot* you would use for tying off the end of something) to numerous complicated knots. Ancient civilizations alone came up with 19 different knots, including the bowline, the bottle sling, the clove hitch, the cat's paw, the Eskimo bowline, the fishermen and the double fishermen, the figure-eight, the overhand, the running bowline, the thief, the reef, and the Turks head knots, along with the Kalmyk loop, the single and half hitch, the two half hitches, the overhand loop, and the one-sided overhand bend. Below are instructions to some of these knots.

Bottle Sling

Instructions:

1. Take a one-foot-long piece of string and fold it in half.
2. Lay the folded string down flat with the two sides parallel to each other. The loop should be at the top and the two open ends at the

bottom.

3. Find the third of the folded string length from the top (the loop) and fold it downward. The loop should lie on top of the parallel strings, creating two "ears".

4. Twist both "ears" towards you and then back down, creating a small twist at their bottom.

5. Put the left "ear" over the right one, and under them, you'll find a small hole.

6. Put your fingers in the hole, and pull it downwards until you make it into a larger, loop.

7. Take this third loop at the bottom, bring it up, and pull it through the other two loops on the top.

8. Pull the third loop upwards, and the other two downwards. The double loop at the bottom goes over a bottleneck.

9. Once you put the double loop on the bottle, you can pull the third loop and the two ends of the string to tighten the loop around the bottle.

10. Tie the strings free ends off, and you'll be left with two small handles on the bottleneck to lift and carry the bottle.

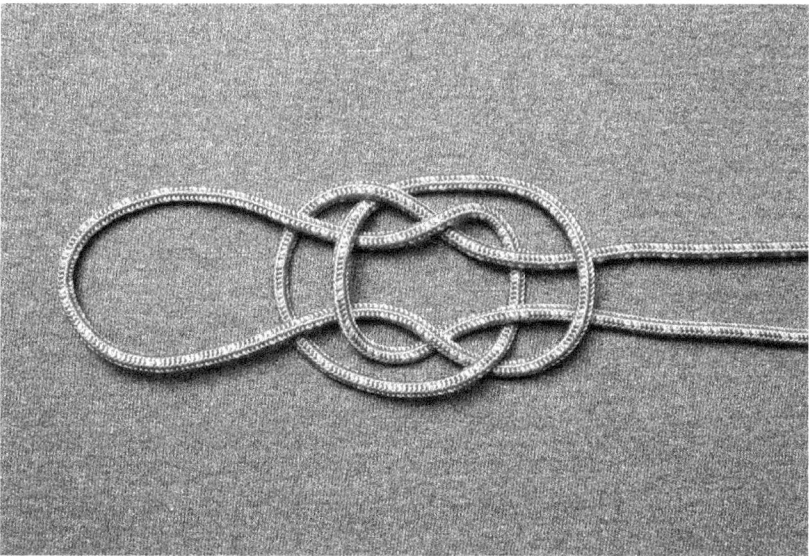

Bottle sling.

Cat's Paw on a Ring
Instructions:
1. Make a loop with your rope and pull it over a ring. The loop should be behind the two strands.
2. Pull the two ends of the rope through the loop.
3. Make the loop in the middle larger by pulling it downwards.
4. Turn the ring away from yourself, into the loop again, and then around, away from yourself.
5. Pull the rope's ends downward while adjusting the loop to tighten it.
6. Work toward the ring until you get a tight knot that looks like a cat's paw underneath it.
7. It makes a nice keychain.

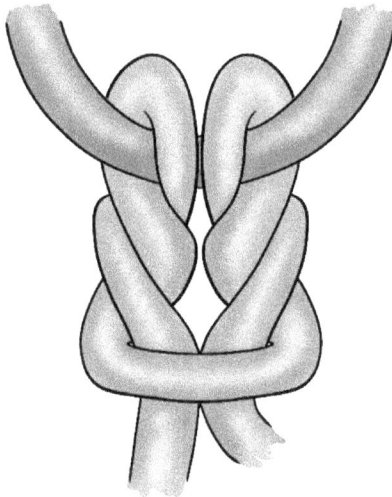

Cat's Paw on a Ring

Eskimo Bowline
Instructions:
1. Lay a piece of string flat and create a loop underneath it by tossing the right end to the left, and then to the right. You've created an overhand loop
2. Take the left end of the string, and place it straight underneath the loop.

3. Take the same end and pull it over the loop, thread it under the straight line you've created in the previous step.

4. Pull the end over the left side of the loop.

5. Grab the loop with your left hand, and the longer end of the rope with your right hand, and gently pull the knot tight. The knot will look similar to a regular bowline except its tied around part of the loop.

6. You can use the Eskimo bowline anytime you want a secure knot in a place where a regular knot can come loose, like tightening equipment when climbing and hiking.

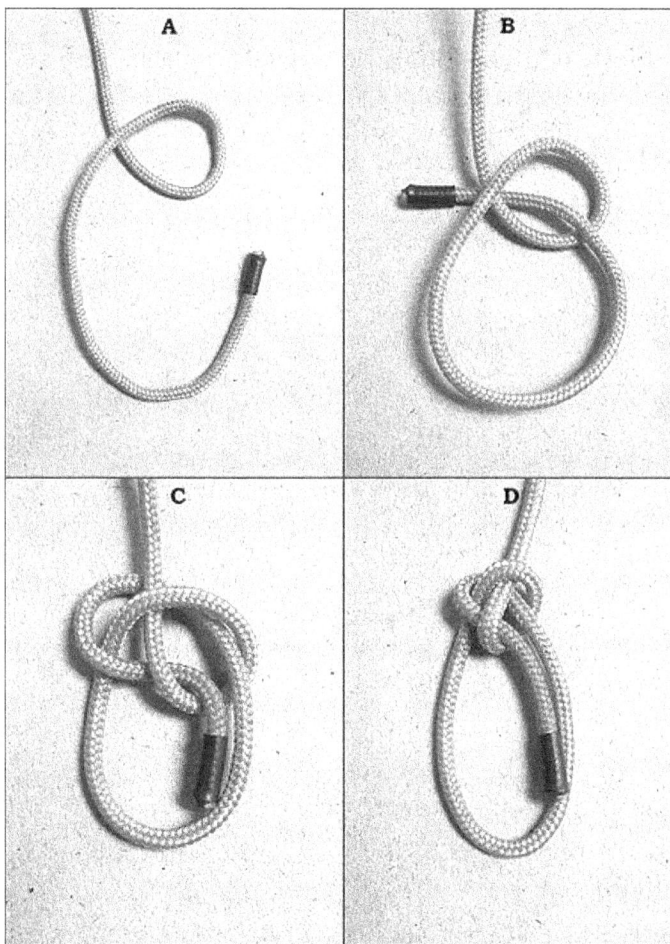

Eskimo Bowline.

FFouche, CC BY-SA 4.0 <https://creativecommons.org/licenses/by-sa/4.0>, via Wikimedia Commons. https://commons.wikimedia.org/wiki/File:Eskimo_Boeglynknoop.jpg

Running Bowline
Instructions:
1. Loop the rope around a pen.
2. Create a bight and pass one of the ropes end over the other. The bight should be under the crossing point of the two ends
3. Thread the rope under the second (non-working) end and through the loop.
4. Pull the working end behind the loop around the pole.
5. Thread it back through the loop
6. Tighten by pulling the ends toward the left.
7. The finished knot is similar to a regular bowline with an extra loop added to it before its tied. Its useful when you want to throw a loop over something you want to catch.

Running bowline.

The Thief
Instructions:
1. Make a bight (loop) at one end of the rope
2. Feed the opposite end of the rope through the loop from under the loop.
3. Pulling this end over the top, loop it back underneath the first loop. After you make the second loop, put the end of the rope on top of it — the two ends of the rope should look in opposite directions.

4. Thread the end of the right side under the loop, and pull both ends tight to finish off the knot.

5. The finished thief knot look like a square knot, except that the loose ends are on the opposite ends of the knot. Its often used to close bags.

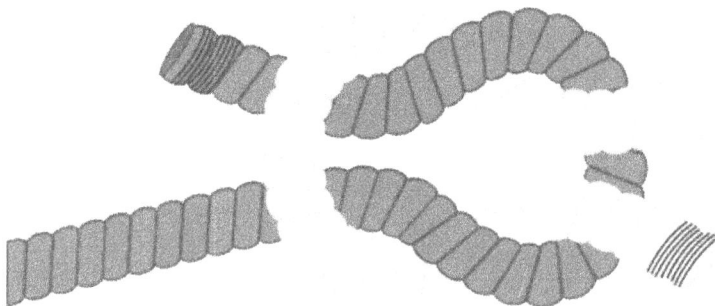

The thief.

Turks Head Knot

Instructions:

1. Fold a piece of paracord in half over a pen.

2. Make a circle around the pen with the paracord by bringing the two ends together and folding them in opposite directions.

3. Pass the left-hand end underneath the right-hand one.

4. Again, pass the left-hand strand and over it over the first loop.

5. Pass the working end underneath the right-hand end.

6. Place the right-hand end over the second loop and pass it under the first loop.

7. Turn over the pen and pass the top loop over the bottom loop.

8. Move the end on the bottom over the bottom loop and under the top loop.

9. Thread the top end under the top loop and pass it over the bottom loop.

10. Pull the knot tight. Once you remove it from a pen the knot has a circular shape. You can use it as a decoration at the end of the pen or any circular object you use.

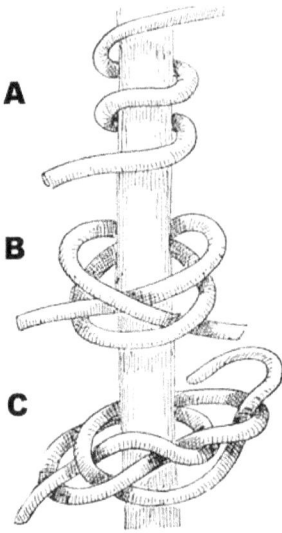

Turks head knot.

The Kalmyk Loop

Instructions:

1. Form a small loop with your string.

2. Pass one end of the string over the top of the loop and pull it under. You now have an inner loop on the left and an outer loop on the right side.

3. From the leftover end on the same side, create a bight (fold the string in half), and pass it over the outer loop and under and up over the inner loop (the original one).

4. Pull the large loop you've created on the right side to tighten the knot.

5. Its similar to the Eskimo bowline, except its tied with a bight, but can be used for the same purposes.

The Kalmyk Loop.

You'll learn about the rest of the knots soon.

Knot tying was also featured in Chinese knotting, made popular by the Tang and Song Dynasties between the 10th and the 13th centuries. By this time, Chinese folk artists used 11 types of knots, including the good luck, the four-flower, the cross, , the double connection, the Chinese button, the double coin, the square, the Pan Chang, the Agemaki, and the Plafond knot. Below are instructions to some of these knots.

Good Luck Knot

Instructions:

1. Fold your cord in half and lay it flat. Pin the top loop down.

2. About four inches from the top of the loop on the right side, form another loop (bight). Pin it down.

3. Repeat step 2 on the left side.

4. Take the loose ends from the bottom and fold them over the left loop. They should be parallel to the top loop, and you should have a small to the bottom left from the center.

5. Move the left loop over the loose ends and the top loop. It should lay around half of the right loop.

6. Move the top loop over the loops on the right.

7. Thread the longer right loop over the small hole from step 4.

8. Tighten the knot by gently tugging on both ends and the loops until you have a square shape at the center.

9. Move the left loop over the bottom one, leaving a small opening between them.

10. Move the bottom loop over the two right loops and onto the right side of the ends.

11. Move the strands over the left loop and thread them through the small opening from step 9.

12. Tighten the loop to create a middle square made of the four quarters. There should be tiny loops on the edges of all quarters and three loops coming from left, right, and top of the square.

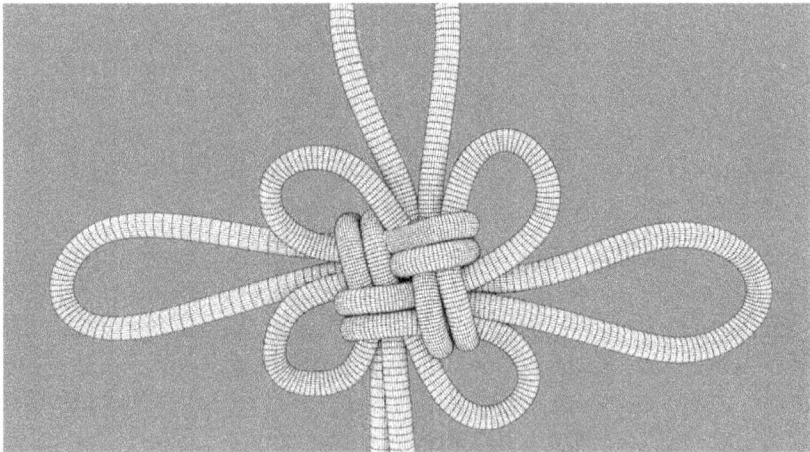

Good luck knot.

Zaripov Rustem, CC BY-SA 4.0 <https://creativecommons.org/licenses/by-sa/4.0>, via Wikimedia Commons. https://commons.wikimedia.org/wiki/File:Good_luck_knot(ABOK_2437).jpg

Four-Flower Knot

Instructions:

1. Take two cords and fold both to create two loops. Cross the loop of the second cord over the loop of the first one.

2. Fold the second loop down and throw the loose strands of the second cord over it to make a knot.

3. You now have one loop and four strands coming from it. Pin the loop down.

4. Pass the third strand over the fourth one, then bring it back from under, creating a knot on the fourth strand.

5. Repeat step 4.

6. Repeat steps 4 and 5 on the other side by passing the second strand over and under the first one two times.

7. Double up the first and fourth strands to make a loop.

8. Thread the third strand through the loop from the previous step and do the same with the second strand.

9. Gently pull all four ends tight. You'll have four small flower shapes in the middle. You can use it for decorations.

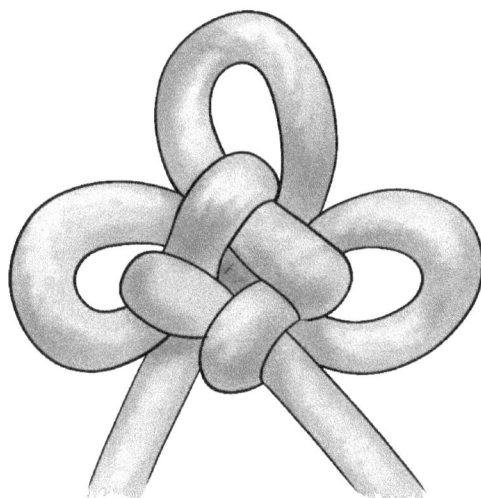

Four-Flower Knot.

Cross

Instructions:

1. Make a loop with your cord.

2. Place the left strand behind the right one to create a second loop on the left, then move the left strand back to the left side to make a third loop on the right.

3. Feed the right strand through the top loop from under. Then, feed it through the right-hand loop from over.

4. Tighten by adjusting the strands.

5. The finished knot has a cross shape on both sides (front and back). Can be used for decorations or tying a tie.

Cross knot.

Double Connection (Double Happiness)

Instructions:

1. Fold your cord and lay the two strands horizontally.

2. Pass the bottom strand over the top one and bring it down under to form a loop.

3. Move the same strand back over the loop you've just created.

4. Close the loop by tightening the strands.

5. Use the other strand to make a loop over the first strand (under the knot you've made in step 4).

6. Then, thread the second strand through the first loop and the one made in the previous step.

7. Tuck on both loops slowly to close the two loops until you get a cross shape in the middle.

8. Often used in ceremonies to celebrate a connection between two people.

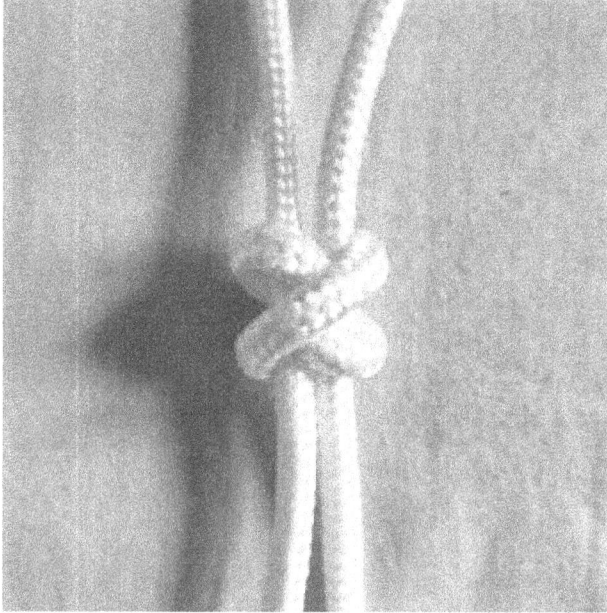

Double Connection.

Pan Chang

Instructions:

1. Prepare a piece of paracord, pins, and a Styrofoam pad (or a similar surface into which you can put your pins).

2. Fold the cord by leaving a little more cord on the left end. You create a bight facing up. Pin it down on the top of the loop.

3. Using the right end of the cord, make a second bight — this one should be facing down.

4. Pin it down, make a third bight on the left end) also facing down) and pin this one as well)

5. Take the right end of the cord, make a bight, and feed this bight first under the outer line, then over the inner line of the second bight (the one you created in step 2.). Continue threading it under the outer line and over the inner line of the original bite.

6. Repeat step 5 to create two horizontal bights. Pin both on the right side.

7. Pin the small squares in the middle and the cords right end.

8. Take the cord's left end threading through the small loop on the top right, under the next four lines, and bring it out at the left side again.

9. Repeat the previous step in the middle (the space between the two horizontal bights from step 6).

10. Thread the cord's left end under the through the opening on the bottom left. Moving upwards on the left side, cross the end over the next three lines, under the next two.

11. Turning back downwards, pass the end through the top left loop, under the next two lines, under one line, under the next three, over one, and finally under the last line to emerge at the bottom.

12. Repeat steps 10 and 11 in the middle (between two vertical bights).

13. Remove the pins and slowly tighten the knot by adjusting the loops one by one.

14. You'll have a flat square knot made of lots of tiny knots. You can use if for decoration, necklaces, key chains, etc.

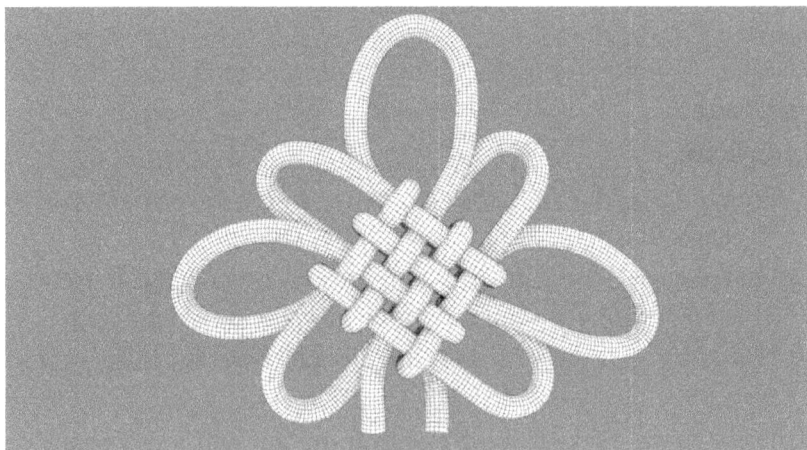

Pan Chang.

Agemaki

Instructions:

1. Take a 3-foot-long cord, take one end, and thread it under and over the top to create an overhand knot.

2. Thread the other hand of the cord through the knot and make another overhand knot. The two knots should be next to each other.

3. Take the inner side of the left knot and pull it through the right knot. At the same time, take the inner side of the right knot and pull it through the left one.

4. You'll have three loops (left, top, and right), and the loose ends on the bottom. Gently pull on all these, adjusting them until you've tightened the intricate Agemaki knot in the middle. The finished knot looks like a dragonfly.

5. Traditionally the knot was used on Samurai armor, but it can be used as a decoration too.

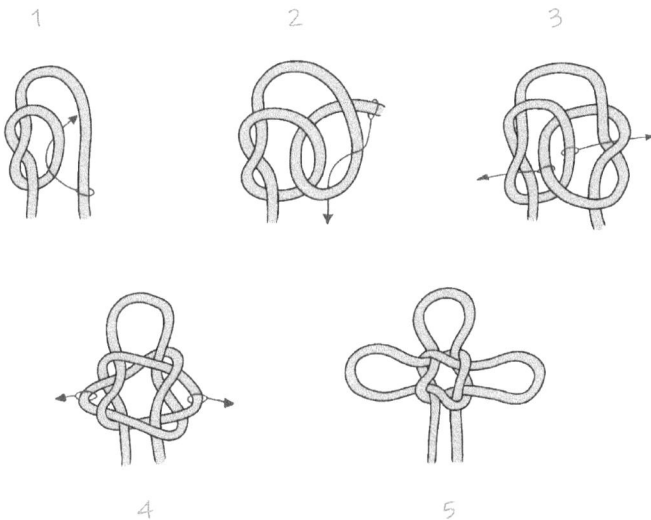

Agemaki.

True Lover's Knot
Instructions:

1. Create an overhand loop.

2. Tuck the working end under the loop and pull it on the top. Tighten it a little bit to create a simple overhand knot.

3. Using the working end of the rope, create another loop over the first one.

4. Thread the rope'

5. s end under the original loop, then loop it back toward the top to create a third loop.
6. Tuck the working end through the third loop to create a second overhand knot.
7. Tighten the right overhand knot first, then tighten the left one as well to finish the true love knot.
8. It looks similar to a square knot (except the strands face different directions) and is used for decorations.

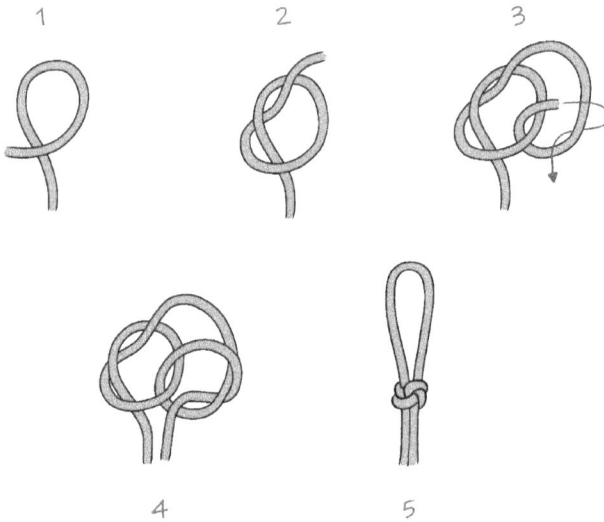

True Lover's Knot.

Plafond Knot
Instructions:
1. Make a loop, then thread one of the strands over it to make a half knot.
2. Make a second half knot under the first one. Tighten this one a little, but leave the first loop big.
3. Leave some space under the second half knot, make a loop, and convert it into a third half knot.
4. Make a fourth half knot under and fold the part with the last two half knots into the middle part.
5. Fold the upper loop on top of the center.

6. Take the top of the upper loop (bight) and feed it through the bottom half knots (the actual knots, not the loops).

7. Feed the left strand through the top two half knots.

8. Thread the right strand through the first strand in the middle, then through the top half knots.

9. Pull on two loose strands and the loop at the top to tighten the knot. You can place it at the end of zippers for decorations and to make move the zipper up and down easier.

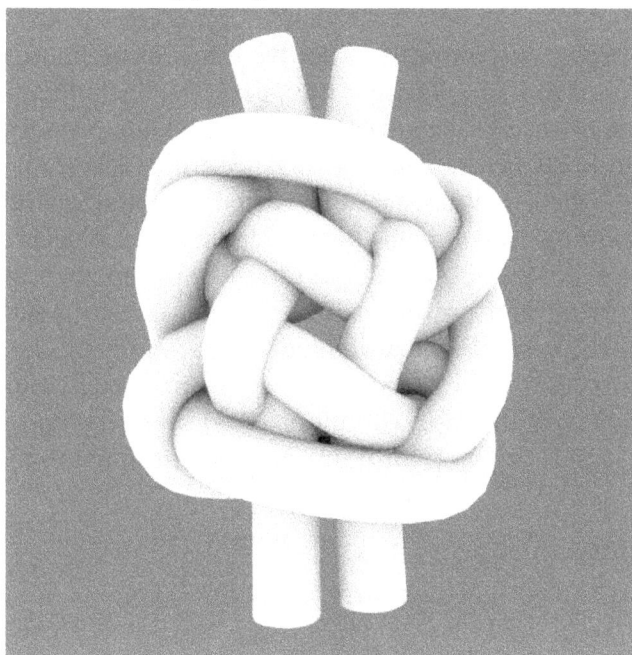

Plafond knot.

Zaripov Rustem, CC BY-SA 4.0 <https://creativecommons.org/licenses/by-sa/4.0>, via Wikimedia Commons. https://commons.wikimedia.org/wiki/File:Plafond_knot.png

You'll learn about the rest later.

In the late 15th century, Europeans discovered another use for knot tying. These were ropewalks . . . long and narrow structures between which they could twist rope and create different forms of knots. During the 15th century, the Incas used knot-tying for recordkeeping. They recorded their calendars and important events in a complex textile system called *Khipu* (or *quipu*), made by intricate knotting.

By the 17th century, knot-tying for different purposes was widespread in Europe, so it's no surprise that it made its way to the courts, too.

Macramé was invented, and Queen Mary the Second and her ladies-in-waiting spent much of their time making different decorations through this unique art form.

Knot tying kept evolving as people kept finding ways to create new knots. Whenever they thought there were no more ways to tie something into a knot, they added another twist or loop and ended up with a new and often more complex structure.

The Revolution of Knot Tying

One of the biggest discoveries in knot tying was using knots in sailboats. Knots were used in many different ways on boats, including for rigging, a system that sailors used to control their vessels. While primitive knots had been used on boats beforehand, the practice truly picked up in the early 19th century, when new uses were invented. Around this time, people started transporting everything by boat, including large objects and animals (as there were no planes, trains, or cars). Tying up the cargo allowed sailors to secure it and prevent it from moving due to a strong tide (or distraction in the case of animals). They would simply tie the knot at the end of the rope they used to secure the items or animals, and they could travel safely. One of the most commonly used knots for this purpose was the bowline knot, a tying form presumably invented by the ancient Egyptians.

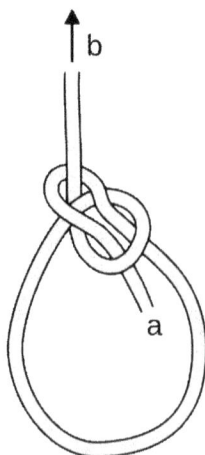

The bowline knot is a tying form presumably invented by the ancient Egyptians.
Helladerivative work: Tescobar, CC BY-SA 2.5 <https://creativecommons.org/licenses/by-sa/2.5>, via Wikimedia Commons: https://commons.wikimedia.org/wiki/File:Bowline_(standard).svg

Sailors and remarkable knot crafters often developed new, more secure structures – many of which are still used today, not just on boats but on other outdoor adventures.

Besides continually inventing new knots to secure things on their ships, sailors also practiced an artistic knotwork called cox-combing. While the main purpose of this knotwork was to decorate the ship, it also served as protection. Some sailors also used coxcomb patterns to identify their ships. Some commonly used cox-combing knots were the Flemish, the French whipping, and the Turk's head knots. While the practice isn't as common as it once was, some modern boaters still place similar knotwork on their rudders, tillers, and wheels.

Sailors also invented the measurement called a knot (known as the sailor's knot today), using it to gauge how fast their ship traveled across the water. They measured this with a device that consisted of a pie-shaped piece of wood and a rope coil with regularly spaced knots across it. By lowering the wood piece into the water, they could track how much of the rope was unraveling during a specific time. When this time passed, they would pull in the rope and count the number of knots on the part that unraveled. The number of knots gave them the boat's speed.

Modern Uses for Knots

While knot use on ships and boats isn't as popular as it was when these vessels were the main transportation methods people used to get around (mainly because modern ships are powered by steam engines and not wind through sails), knot tying has found its way into many other areas of life.

Besides using them in recreational sailing and other outdoor adventures, you may have already encountered a few examples of knot-tying without even realizing it. For example, have you ever seen someone tie a necktie or make a knitted sweater? Even sewn pieces of cloth can have elements that require tying together or serving as decorations.

Basket weavers and rug knitters also use knot tying to create their pieces. Girls with long hair often wear intricate braids, which can include knots. And, if you're an outdoor adventurer, you've probably encountered (or will in the future) many different types of knots as they are used for securing equipment during camping, fishing, mountaineering, rock climbing, hiking, and many other purposes.

Beyond making the trip more enjoyable, knowing how to secure a knot can be a lifesaver during wilderness adventures. You may need knots to attach ropes together so you and your equipment remain secure and avoid losing an essential piece you'll need later (like food, water, first-aid, camping equipment, flashlights, etc.).

Another popular use of knot tying is in macramé, which innovative crafters re-popularized in the 1970s. Some commonly used knots in macramé are the overhand knot (this one truly has many uses), the square knot, the clove hitch, the spiral stitch, and the Lark's head knot.

Spiral Stitch

Instructions:

1. Make two Lark's head knots with two separate strings on a pen.
2. Pass the first strand over the second and third strands and under the fourth strand.
3. Pass the fourth strand under the third and second strands and over the first strand.
4. Tighten the knot you've created, then repeat steps 2 and 3 on the same side several times. Your pattern will take a spiral form naturally.

Spiral stitch.

The other common macramé knots will be described later in the book.

Macramé pieces are typically fashioned with cotton rope, which comes in many colors. Just like in other uses, knot tying in macramé has expanded vastly. This way, all generations can enjoy it. Unlike its original version, which only included intricate designs, the modern version often has wooden or plastic beads, crystals, and other small objects added to it.

As you can see, knots are a versatile tool with numerous functions in people's lives. You can use them for essential functions as people have done since the beginning of time, in outdoor adventures, in crafty hobbies, or for other purposes – the choices are virtually limitless.

The Meaning of Knots in Different Cultures

Beyond practical or decorative purposes, knots have a distinctive meaning in different cultures across the globe.

Celtic Symbols

The Celtic knot is one of their most well-known emblems.

The ancient Celts fondly used different symbols to express their religious beliefs, ideas, and discoveries. The Celtic knot is one of their most well-known emblems; it may be found in Celtic art and historical objects such as the Book of Kells, a text whose cover is decorated with elaborate knot work. The Celtic cross was also originally designed as a form of knot symbolizing the sun god.

Notable Celtic knots include the Triquetra, often known as the Trinity Knot. Its three distinct sections, representing the sacred sequence of threes in the Celtic culture, are created from one continuous line. The ancients believed that good things came in threes and tied the number to many things you'll see in nature, including the moon's phases.

Have you heard the phrase "tying the knot?" It's used when two people get married because, in ancient times, the bride and groom had their hands tied together as part of their wedding ceremony. This practice hails from the Celtic culture, where it was called handfasting (some still use these kinds of ceremonies today). The couple was asked to take each other's hand while a third person tied their hands with a cord or a ribbon so they would look like a knot. Different colors were used to symbolize what the couple promised to each other (for example, blue ribbons meant trust and devotion), much like newlyweds express this to each other in their vows.

Egyptian Symbolism

In ancient Egypt, knots were seen as a symbol of infinite paths and firm connections. Both symbols come from the Egyptian's reverence for their gods and goddesses. Different knots were used to represent the eternal life of deities in ceremonies held in their honor and to celebrate those with good values.

Chinese Symbolism

The Chinese used knots in weddings, and knotwork is still featured in modern ceremonies.
Ucla90024, CC BY-SA 3.0 <https://creativecommons.org/licenses/by-sa/3.0>, via Wikimedia Commons: https://commons.wikimedia.org/wiki/File:Chinese_Knot_P4R.jpg

Like the ancient Celts, the Chinese also used knots in weddings, and knotwork is still featured in modern ceremonies. The double happiness and true love knots are still among the most often used knots in Chinese weddings. Couples can also gift artwork containing these knots to each other before their wedding.

In Chinese culture, knots (particularly the red ones) are seen as symbols of good fortune. In ancient times, if a Chinese family wanted to chase away bad luck from their lives, they would decorate their house with red-knotted artwork. They believed that by keeping misfortune away, they left room for good luck to come into their home. Other knots in Chinese culture are used for protection in dangerous situations or when they believe someone wants to cause harm to another. And just like they had knots for unity, the Chinese also used knotwork to represent freedom.

Section 2: Getting Started

Knot tying is a basic skill that anyone can learn. It may not seem like it, but you'll notice that there are many times when tying a knot is useful – for both fun and serious work. It helps to know about many kinds of knots and when to use them because you can quickly be thrown into the deep end, where you have to think on your feet. When the situation arises, and a skilled person who knows how to tie knots is called forward, you will be the savior who steps up and knows exactly what to do!

Knots are for the adventurer who spends a lot of time outdoors. Whether camping, fishing, or mountain climbing, not knowing much about knots may leave you struggling at the wrong moments. So, one of the first steps toward becoming a survival expert and a handy person is knowing the basics. Once you have mastered the basics, you can move on to more complicated knots to impress your friends and family. Get ready to jump into the incredible world of knot tying and unleash a whole new skill set that will help make you the coolest person in the woods – and anywhere a rope is around.

Knots are used on boats, as well as securing plants and trees.

Beyond being outside, tying knots will help you in many situations around the house or on the road. For example, if you plan to move a lot of goods on a pick-up truck, it may be necessary to tie down the items so they don't fall off along the way. You might one day find yourself having to tow a friend who got stuck on the side of the road. Knowing a strong knot will ensure the car is safely secured.

Knots are often used in gardening to secure trees or various plants into position. Knots are used in construction to secure equipment, building materials, and boats. So, as you get older, you'll find more use for what you've learned in this book. Best to start learning now to stay ahead of the game and never be caught off guard by a tricky situation!

Basic Knot Tying Kit: Tools and Materials Needed for Knot Tying

Every adventure expert says a strong rope is super important to have in your backpack when you go hiking. Builders and mechanics also love ropes because they can do so many helpful things on the job or in a garage. Knowing about different ropes and tools makes you a cool knot-tying hero!

It's really smart to have a rope and knot-tying kit ready for emergencies. With a rope and some gadgets like hooks, clips, and pulleys, you can make awesome tools to help you out. Need to lift something heavy by yourself? A pulley can make it easy-peasy. Want to hang a hammock in the forest or keep your stuff safe from animals by tying it up in a tree? Or maybe you need to keep things tied down at a building site or fix something quickly at home. These are all times when your knot-tying kit comes in handy. You can carry your kit in a small bag or leave it in your family's car. With the right skills and gear, you'll be ready to solve any problem with a rope and your smart knot ideas.

Types of Rope

Ropes are super important for tying knots - the star of your knot-tying kit! You can skip some tools, but you definitely need rope because no rope means no knots. There are lots of different ropes for different tasks, and here's a quick guide to some of them:

- **Cotton Rope:** Good for gardening and decorating your room. It's nice to the planet, but it doesn't like getting wet because it gets heavier and can break easily.
- **Nylon Rope:** Outdoor adventurers love this one! It's super strong, bends well, and can carry heavy stuff without a sweat.
- **Manila Rope:** Made from plants, it's fantastic for garden work but doesn't like water too much - it shrinks and can break after a while.
- **Polypropylene Rope:** Builders and boat lovers use this because it's light, tough, and even floats on water.
- **Polyester Rope:** Really strong and doesn't stretch or mind the heat. Great for tying things down securely or for flagpoles.
- **HMPE Rope:** Superhero strong - even stronger than steel! Perfect for outdoor adventures because it ties really good knots.

Each type of rope has its own special job, so pick the right rope for your adventure or project!

Clip

Clips can either be made of plastic or metal. Specialized clips like carabiners are used in rock climbing. This versatile tool allows you to attach ropes to many different items in unique ways.

Pulley

A pulley is a wheel that a rope passes over. Pulleys help decrease the weight of items, and they can be used in different combinations to make lifting and moving heavy items easier.

Ring

Rings are simple metal circles that you can use to tie objects in different ways. The ring's simple design allows it to be used creatively in many scenarios and is a handy tool to keep with you.

Scissors

Sometimes, you must cut a rope shorter, or you may have no choice but to snip a tangled mess. A scissor is a simple tool everybody has around the house that can always be useful when tying knots or working with rope.

Cleat

A cleat is a T-shaped object usually made of wood or metal. This tool is secured to a flat surface for you to tie a rope around. You will see cleats at docks for people to tie their boats down.

Hook

A hook is a curved piece of metal used to hang objects on. Keeping some screw-in hooks nearby can be helpful in many situations where you need to secure something or hang objects on it.

Practical Applications of Knots

Knowing just one or two knots isn't enough because different adventures need different types of knots! Think about it: you use a knot daily to tie your shoes before heading out. Knots are super handy for tying things together, carrying heavy stuff, and keeping things in place.

Some knots are easy to untie when needed, and some are super strong and won't loosen up, no matter what. With all the knots you can learn, you'll always find the perfect one for what you're doing, whether you need to keep something tied tight or gently lower something heavy to the ground.

Knots are not just for one thing; they're used everywhere - from homes to the great outdoors – and even in all kinds of jobs. This book will make you a knot-tying champ, ready for any situation, whether you're by a lake, in the ocean, on land, building something, or out camping or hunting. Knots helped people build amazing things and are a super cool skill that's been a bit forgotten. But once you dive into the world of knots, you'll see how awesome and important they really are!

Basic Knot Terminology

When you start learning to tie knots, the instructions will use common words. Without understanding the meanings of these words, you could quickly become lost, causing a lot of unnecessary struggle. The words listed below will help you sound like you know what you are talking about and allow you to follow instructions correctly.

Bight

This describes the part of the rope that is between the two ends. It is mainly used to discuss any curved section on a rope that has not been tied.

Loop

Once two parts of your rope cross each other, the bight will now become a loop. A loop will either be overhand or underhand, depending on the positioning of your standing part. If the working end goes over your standing part, it is an *overhand* loop; if it goes under your standing part, it is an *underhand* loop.

Crossing Point

The crossing point is where two sections of your rope cross to form a loop.

Working End

The working end is the section of the rope you are handling to tie the knot.

Standing Part

The standing part is also known as the standing end. This is the end of the rope you are not actively using to tie a knot.

Practice, Practice, and Practice

When you first start tying knots, it will be difficult. You may have to keep looking over the instructions and moving slowly. The more you practice, the faster and better you will become! If you work on your rope-tying skills, you will be ready when the time comes to put them to use. It does not help just reading about different kinds of knots and their uses. You must get out there and get your hands dirty.

Test Your Skills and Knowledge

1. What is a *pulley*, and what can it be used for?

2. If you were making a rope-tying kit, which items would you include?

3. Why is it important to always carry a rope with you if you are going out into the wilderness?

4. List five uses of ropes you could see applied in your everyday life.

5. What is a "bight"?

6. What does the "loop" refer to when tying a knot?

7. What does "working end" refer to when tying a knot?

8. Which part of the rope is the *standing end* when tying a knot?

9. How can a pair of scissors be helpful when you need to tie a knot?

10. Name three types of ropes and their uses.

Section 3: Basic Knots

Now that you've picked up some cool knot words and what they're for, you're all set to start tying! Remember, learning to tie knots is like learning to walk before you can run. First up, we'll cover the basics. You might know some of these knots already, and some might be totally new to you. Start with these simple ones, and soon, you'll be ready for more tricky knots that use the same ideas.

Even though these first knots are for beginners, they're super useful in lots of different ways. You'll learn how to tie them and where – and why – they're handy. But don't stop there! Once you've got the hang of them, try your own ideas. Learning knots is all about getting creative with ropes and strings. So, if you think a knot could work somewhere else, go for it and try it out. These basics will help you see rope in a whole new way – not just as a piece of string but as an awesome tool for all kinds of tasks and fun.

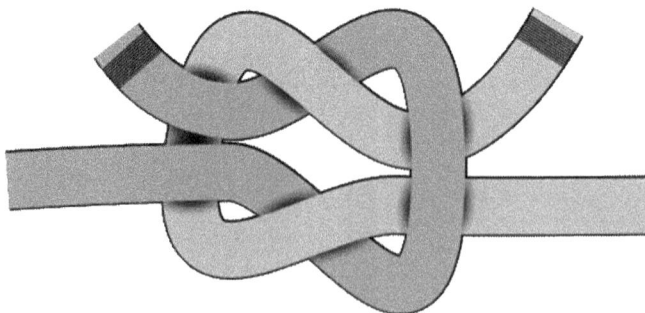

Square knot.
https://commons.wikimedia.org/wiki/File:Platteknoop.svg

Square Knot

The square knot is one of the first techniques people learn because it is used for the laces on our shoes. The square knot is also known as a reef knot because it was once used to secure sails in rough winds. This knot works amazingly for tying bundles together, so it can be used both in the home and outdoors. The square knot has even been used to tie bandages tightly if the blood from a wound needs to be stopped quickly. This simple knot is easy to learn and can come in handy in many scenarios if you use your imagination.

How to Tie a Square Knot:

1. Grab hold of the two ends of a rope.
2. Take the end in one hand and cross it over the end in your other hand.
3. Then, take the end you have crossed over on the top and wrap it around the bottom.
4. Now, take both ends of the rope and repeat the same process of wrapping one end around the other.
5. Pull both ends to tighten.

Bowline Knot

The bowline knot creates a fixed loop at the end of your cordage. So, you'll have a line with a circle at the end of it. The loop is not adjustable, so you need to determine the size before tightening the knot. The rope will be secured tightly and will not slip at all. This knot can support a lot of weight, and it is easy to untie even after having carried a heavy load. This knot has been used for rock climbing and in rescue missions. It originated on sailboats and was used to secure the anchors and sails. The bowline knot is your best option for any situation where you need an immovable loop at the end of your cordage.

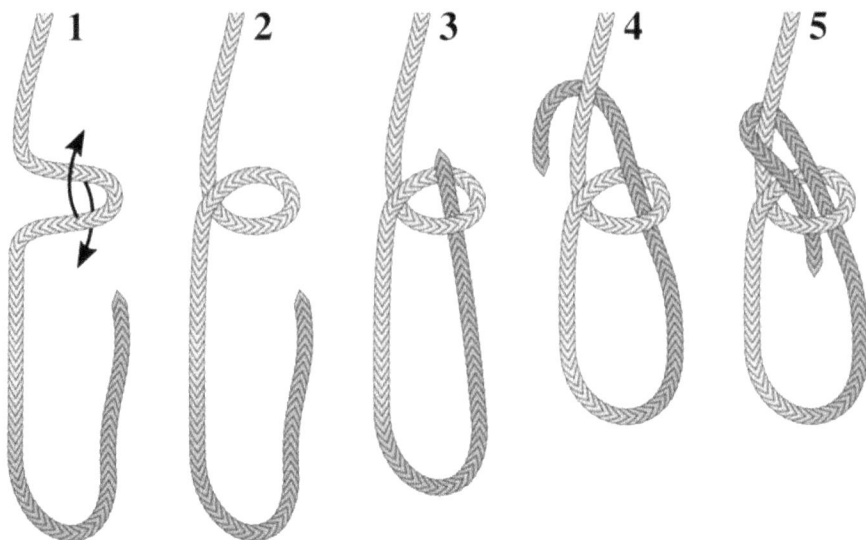

Bowline knot.

How to Tie a Bowline Knot:

1. Start by creating a loop.

2. Take the working end of your cordage, wrap it around the bottom of the loop, and then thread it through the center of the hole you have created. You should now have two loops – the smaller, original loop and the second, bigger one you have just made.

3. Grab the working end you have threaded through the first smaller loop and wrap it underneath the standing end.

4. Take the working end and thread it back through the original loop.

5. Then, pull on the standing end and working end to tighten the knot.

Bowline on a Bight

This is a variation of the bowline knot that you have just learned. This knot is a little more complicated, but if you follow the instructions carefully, you can master it without much effort. This knot allows you to create a loop in any section of the rope if the end is not available or does not work for what you want to achieve. The loop created by the bowline on a bight has been used for a toe hold in emergencies and also for climbing. Like a traditional bowline, the support knot is strong. It won't slip, but it is easy to untie.

How to Tie a Bowline on a Bight:

1. Grab a double section of rope to form a loop.

2. Take the working end and push it through the center of the loop.

3. Separate the working end by bringing it to the bottom of your double loop.

4. Thread the double loop through the eye you have created by separating the sections of the working end.

5. Hold the standing end and pull on the double loop to tighten the knot.

Granny Knot

The granny knot is similar to the square knot, so it is usually used to tie bundles together or a rope onto an object. The knot isn't as strong as the square knot, so it is not used as often. Most of the time, you would opt to use the square knot instead of the granny knot, but it helps to have several options. You cannot use a granny knot to secure two ropes because it can easily become undone with a heavy load. This knot is often used for jewelry or for bracelets.

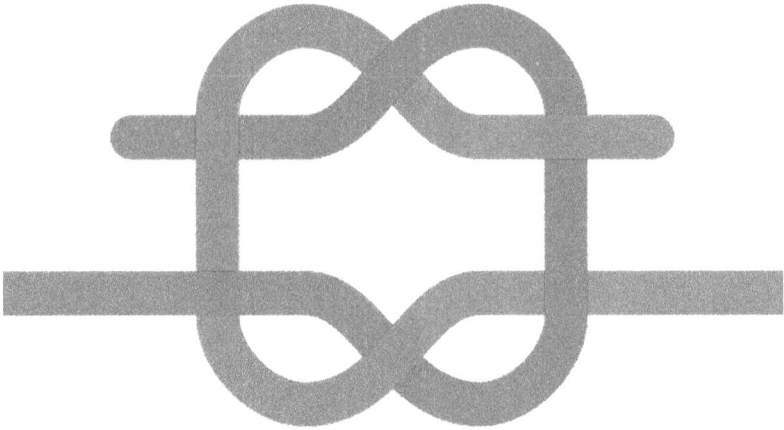

Granny knot.
https://commons.wikimedia.org/wiki/File:Granny_knot.svg

How to Tie a Granny Knot:

1. Start by overlapping two ends of your cordage.

2. Fold over one section of your cordage, pass it over, and then put it through the other end.

3. Pass the opposite end through the loop you have created and pull to tighten.

Figure 8 Knot

The figure 8 is also known as a Flemish knot. Climbers often use this knot as a stopper because it will jam against a cord, which helps to block it. The knot can be easily undone, and it is used so that a climber can quickly untie it as they move swiftly up the mountain to the tippy-top. You should be careful when using this knot as a stopper that takes too much weight because, under great pressure, it can become undone. This knot is a chunky double layer the end of it.

How to Tie a Figure 8 Knot:

1. Pass your working end over your standing end to form a loop.

2. Lift up and move the working end beneath and around the standing end.

3. Then, pass the working end over and through the original loop you created.

4. Pull to tighten.

Slip Knot

A slip knot is also used as a stopper, much like the figure 8 knot, because it is easy to untie. This knot is also used in knitting and in crochet projects. A slip knot can also be applied for hauling or trapping because it tightens as you pull on it. The knot can also be utilized to secure objects, but it should not take on a heavy load because it might come loose.

Slip knot.

How to Tie a Slip Knot:

1. Fold your cordage to create an open loop.

2. Grab your working end, create another loop, and then run the end over the two parallel lines you have created with your first open loop.

3. After taking the working end over the two sections of the standing line, wrap it under the line and thread it through the second loop you created.

4. Wrap it around the two sections and through the second loop another two times before pulling on the loop and the working end to tighten it.

5. You should then be able to slide the knot up or down to extend or shrink the loop.

Half Hitch

This knot is used to secure a rope against a solid object, like a pole or a tree. It can tie down valuables you don't want to lose in a wilderness environment. This knot is also great for securing a tent or putting up a clothesline in the yard.

Half hitch.

https://commons.wikimedia.org/wiki/File:Halvesteek.svg

How to Tie a Half Hitch:

1. Start by wrapping your rope around a column to form a bight.

2. Grab your working end and cross it over your standing end to form a loop around the column.

3. Thread the working end through your loop underneath the standing end.

4. Pull to tighten before taking your working end back over your loop and around the column to form another loop.

5. Tuck the working end underneath the standing end and thread it back through the new loop you created.

6. Pull on the working end to tighten.

Two Half Hitches

This knot is a form of the half hitch, and it can be applied in many situations. This strong knot is secure, but it can also be easily untied. You can use this knot to put a swing up in the yard or as a bucket handle. Much like the half hitch, it is excellent for securing objects to a solid column. The knot looks almost like a pretzel.

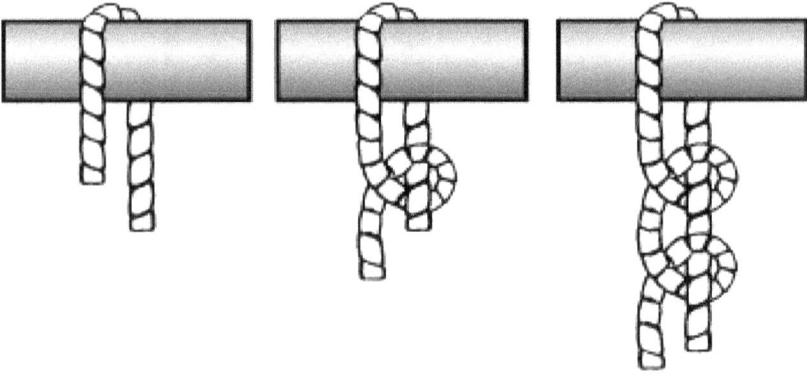

How to Tie Two-Half Hitches:

1. Create a loop by wrapping your rope around a pole.
2. Next, make a half hitch by passing your working end under your loop.
3. To create another half hitch, wrap the working end around the rope.
4. This variation is slightly more secure than your standard half hitch.

Overhand Knot

The overhand knot is extremely solid to the point that it can sometimes be a disadvantage because it will jam and can be difficult to untie. When using this knot, you should be sure that you want to tie it permanently, or else you will risk having to cut your cordage. This knot can be used to seal up parcels or to secure items that you have no reason to move. You can tie this knot at the end of your cordage to prevent it from fraying. This is one of the first knots many people learn to tie.

How to Tie an Overhand Knot:

1. Start by creating a loop.
2. Thread your working end underneath the standing end.
3. Lastly, thread the working end through the loop before pulling it to tighten.

Test Your Skills and Knowledge

1. Which simple knot is used when you tie your shoelaces?
2. Name one use of a bowline knot.
3. Why is it important to know how to tie a variety of knots?
4. Name two knots that can be used as stoppers.
5. Why is using a square knot better than a granny knot?
6. What is another name for a figure 8 knot?
7. What can a slip knot be used for?
8. Choose one of the knot variations you have learned that seems complicated, and try it with some cordage you have nearby.
9. Which knots do climbers make use of?
10. Which knot would you use if you want to tie two ropes of different thicknesses together?

Section 4: Nautical Knots

Nautical knots are the backbone of sailing, boating, and maritime activities. These knots ensure vessel safety, security, and functionality. From securing lines to preventing accidents and damage, the importance of these knots cannot be overstated. Learning about these knots will make your seagoing adventures fun and practical.

Nautical knots are the backbone of maritime activities.

Ensuring Safety

The primary objective of nautical knots is to contribute to the vessel's safety and everyone on board. Well-tied knots prevent lines from coming loose, which is particularly crucial during adverse weather conditions or challenging situations at sea.

Mastery of Basic Nautical Knots

Sailing the seas is way cooler when you know some basic nautical knots. These knots help with everything from tying your boat to the dock to making loops that can do all sorts of handy things. Plus, learning these knots is not just useful but also pretty fun and good for your brain, helping you get better at moving your hands and fingers just right.

Why Nautical Knots Rock:

- They're essential for doing all sorts of important boat stuff like anchoring and managing sails.
- Knowing the right knot for the job makes everything safer and smoother on the water.

Knots and Culture:

- Tying knots is a big deal in sea culture, with some knots being special to certain places or boats.
- Sharing knot skills is a cool way to keep the sea's traditions alive and feel connected to other sailors from the past and present.

Spotlight on the Clove Hitch: This knot is super handy and easy to tie, great for securing stuff on boats or even making a quick handle. It's simple but really strong.

The Clove Hitch knot is super handy and easy to tie.
Cobanyastigi, CC0, via Wikimedia Commons:

How to Tie a Clove Hitch:

1. Wrap the rope around something sturdy, like a post.

2. Cross the rope over itself to make an 'X.'

3. Wrap it around again the same way.

4. Slip the end under the last wrap to lock it in place. Make sure the end comes out on the opposite side from where it started.

Learning these knots makes you part of a cool tradition and gives you some serious skills for your next sea adventure!

The Cleat Hitch: A Sailor's BFF

22 is perfect for tying a rope to those T-shaped things on docks and boats (those are called cleats). It's strong, easy to tie, and super important for keeping boats where they should be.

How to Tie It:

1. Start by looping the rope around the bottom part of the cleat, away from where the rope will be pulled.
2. Cross the rope over to the other side of the cleat.
3. Make a figure-eight around the two arms of the cleat for extra hold.
4. Finish by looping the rope around one arm of the cleat to keep it in place.

This knot is all about using friction to keep the rope from moving. The more loops you make, the stronger it will hold. It's easy to untie, too, which is great for when you need to move your boat quickly.

Uses and Tips:

- Super for docking boats.
- Keep the tension even while wrapping to make sure the knot stays strong.

Knowing how to tie a Cleat Hitch makes boat docking and securing ropes a breeze. Just remember to loop, cross, and wrap it tight!

The Cool Sheet Bend Knot

The Sheet Bend is an awesome knot that's great at tying together two ropes, even if they're different sizes or types. It's easy to tie, really strong, and super handy in lots of situations.

How to Tie It:

1. Make a loop (like a little U) in the thicker rope.
2. Take the thinner rope and push it up through the loop.
3. Wrap the thinner rope around the loop and back under itself.
4. Pull the end of the thinner rope tight while holding the rest of the ropes. Now you've got a tight and secure knot!

The Sheet Bend is perfect for when you need to tie ropes together that aren't the same, and it stays strong when there's a lot of pull on it. Plus, it's easy to untie, which is great when you need to change things up quickly.

The Anchor Bend Knot: A Sailor's Best Friend

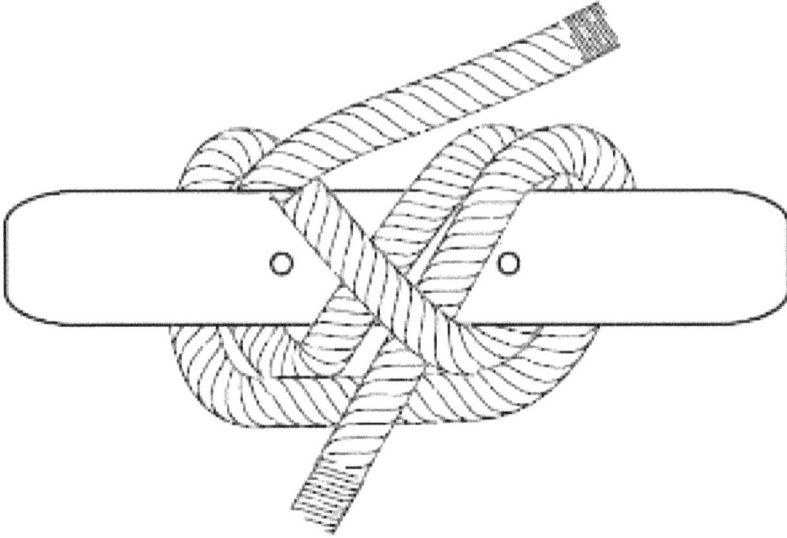

The Anchor Bend knot is super strong – perfect for tying a rope to an anchor or chain.
Quatrostein, CC BY-SA 3.0 <https://creativecommons.org/licenses/by-sa/3.0>, via Wikimedia Commons: https://commons.wikimedia.org/wiki/File:Kikkersteek.png

The Anchor Bend knot is super strong – perfect for tying a rope to an anchor or chain. It's good at holding tight and handling sudden tugs, making it a top choice for anchoring boats safely.

How to Tie It:

1. Make a small loop at the end of your rope.
2. Wrap the end around the main part of the rope and the loop a few times.
3. Tuck the end back through the wraps and pull everything tight. Now you've got a super strong connection!

Why It's Awesome:

- It's great at spreading out the pull on the rope, which means less breakage risk.
- Perfect for when the sea gets choppy, and the anchor moves around a lot.

Staying Safe on the Water: Tying your boat or anchor the right way is super important. If not done correctly, it could lead to accidents, like your boat floating away or bumping into things. Here's why getting your knots right matters:

- **Avoiding Oops Moments:** If a boat isn't tied up properly, it could drift off and cause a mess, like bumping into other boats or the dock.

- **Chill Anchoring:** When you drop anchor in a nice spot, using the Anchor Bend keeps your boat from moving too much, so you can relax or swim without worry.

- **Teamwork Makes the Dream Work:** In races, quickly changing your sails using knots like the Sheet Bend can help you adjust to the wind fast and keep you safe.

Learning knots like the Anchor Bend can make your boating safer and more fun, letting you enjoy the water without stress.

Kayaking and Knots: Keeping Paddles Safe

When kayaking, using figure-eight knots on paddle leashes is super smart. These knots act like stoppers, so your paddle doesn't slip away into the river if things get wild. This ensures your important gear stays with you, letting you focus on the adventure without worrying about losing anything important.

Knots in Sea Stories and Teamwork

Sailors have some cool traditions with knots. For example, wearing a Turk's Head knot on your wrist is like having a lucky charm for protection at sea. These traditions show how special and meaningful knots can be in the sailing world.

Working together to learn knots can also help sailors become closer as a team and feel connected to the long history of sea exploration, where knots were key for staying safe.

Learning how to tie knots right is super important. It keeps everyone safe on the water, avoids mishaps, and keeps the spirit of sailing alive. It's not just about tying ropes; it's about being part of a team and respecting the sea's challenges and traditions.

Section 5: Knots for Outdoor Adventures

When engaging in outdoor activities like climbing, camping, or bushcraft, having a solid grasp of essential skills, particularly knot tying, is paramount. This section focuses on fundamental climbing knots, each crucial in ensuring safety and practicality during various outdoor adventures.

Climbing knot.

Climbing Knots for Safe Adventures

Knowing climbing knots is important for having fun and staying safe on hiking and climbing trips. Let's check out some key knots that you'll want to know:

Bachmann Knot

This one's great for moving up ropes or rocks smoothly. It helps you climb without slipping back down. The Bachmann knot is perfect for climbers needing a dependable friction hitch. Used for ascending or descending ropes, it's sturdy, adjustable, and simple to untie.

How to Tie It:

1. Create a loop in the rope, ensuring it's big enough to fit around your harness or attachment point.

2. Pass the loop underneath the main rope and then wrap it around the main rope once more, forming a double wrap.

3. Thread the loop through itself, making sure it passes over the wraps you've created.

4. Pull both ends of the rope to tighten the knot securely onto the main rope.

Tips:

- Ensure you make tight and secure double wraps around the main rope.
- Easily slide the knot up or down the rope as needed by releasing tension.
- To untie, release tension and push the loop through the wraps.
- Practice tying and untying until you're confident in your ability to tie it correctly.

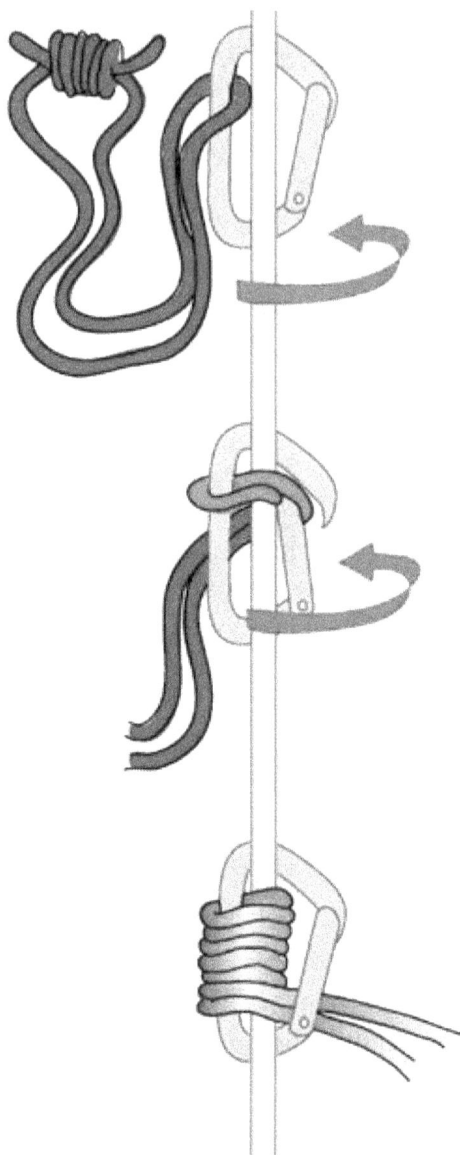

The Bachmann knot is great for moving up ropes or rocks smoothly.
https://commons.wikimedia.org/wiki/File:Bachmann_knot2.png

Klemheist Knot

If you need to climb up a rope or get yourself out of a tricky spot, the Klemheist Knot is your go-to. It's awesome for making sure you can pull yourself up easily. Its gripping capability makes it ideal for ascending or descending ropes, as well as for securing loads or creating makeshift handles.

How to Tie It:

1. Start by forming a small loop in the rope, leaving enough slack for the desired grip size.

2. Pass the loop behind the main rope and then bring it back over itself to form a simple loop.

3. Wrap the loop around the main rope several times, typically 3 to 5 wraps depending on the thickness of the rope and the desired grip strength.

4. Pass the working end of the loop through the initial loop you created.

5. Pull both ends of the rope to cinch the knot tight against the main rope.

The Klemheist knot relies on friction to hold onto the main rope securely. You can easily adjust the position of the knot along the main rope by loosening and sliding it to the desired location. To release the knot, simply push the wraps down the main rope, allowing them to loosen and the knot to untie.

Always perform safety checks to ensure the knot is tied correctly and securely before relying on it for support or load-bearing tasks.

Klemheist Knot.

Autoblock Knot

The Autoblock knot, also known as the French Prusik, is a crucial knot in the arsenal of climbers. It's a backup or safety knot, providing friction and security on a climbing rope. This knot comes handy in situations where climbers need to secure themselves while belaying or rappelling.

How to Tie It:

1. Begin by forming a small loop in the rope, leaving enough slack for the desired grip size.
2. Pass the loop behind the main rope and then bring it back over itself to form a simple loop.
3. Wrap the loop around the main rope several times, usually 4 to 6 wraps depending on the thickness of the rope and the desired friction.
4. Pass the working end of the loop through the initial loop you created, creating a girth hitch around the main rope.
5. Pull both ends of the rope to cinch the knot tight against the main rope, ensuring the wraps are snug and secure.
6. To release the knot, simply push the wraps down the main rope, allowing them to loosen and the knot to untie.

Always perform safety checks to ensure the knot is tied correctly and securely before relying on it for support.

The Autoblock knot.
Cobanyastigi, CC0, via Wikimedia Commons:
https://commons.wikimedia.org/wiki/File:AutoblockBagi.JPG

Double Fisherman's Knot

Need to tie two ropes together? The Double Fisherman's Knot is super strong and reliable, perfect for making longer ropes or creating strong anchor points. Its strength and security make it popular in climbing, mountaineering, and other outdoor activities where reliable connections are essential.

How to Tie It:

1. Lay the two ends of the ropes parallel to each other, overlapping by at least a foot.

2. Take one end and wrap it around both ropes, passing it under and then over both ropes. Repeat this wrapping motion three times, ensuring each wrap is snug and parallel to the others.

3. After completing the wraps, thread the working end through the three wraps from the same direction. This creates a loop around both ropes.

4. Now, take the other end of the rope and repeat the wrapping process in the opposite direction. Wrap it around both ropes, passing it under and then over both ropes three times.

5. After completing the wraps, thread this end through the three wraps from the opposite direction. Ensure the knot is tight and secure.

6. Pull both ends of the ropes simultaneously to tighten the knot securely. Ensure the wraps are neat and snug against the ropes.

Learning to tie the double Fisherman's knot is essential for anyone involved in activities that require joining ropes together securely. With its strength and reliability, it's a knot that climbers and outdoor enthusiasts depend on in critical situations.

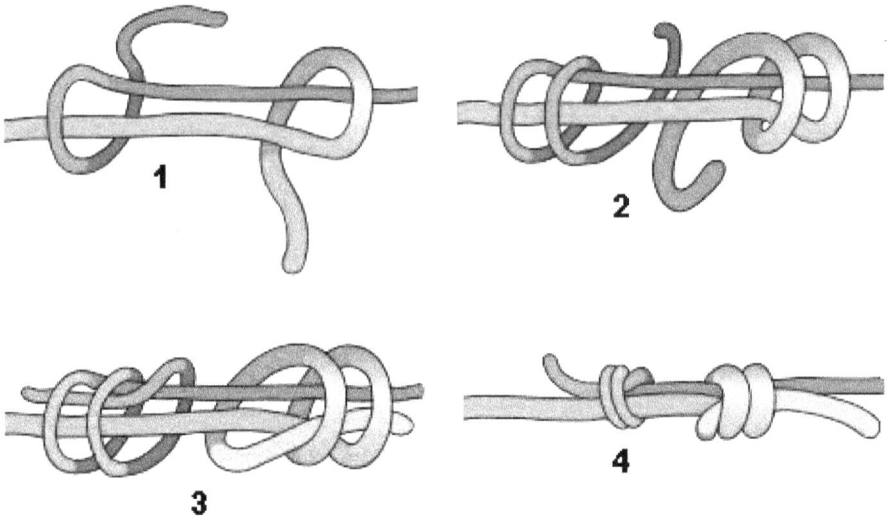

Figure-Eight Knot

This is a basic but super important knot for tying into your harness or making loops in your rope. It's easy to learn and really secure. It's primarily used to create a secure stopper at the end of a rope, preventing it from sliding through a belay device or anchor point. Its simplicity and reliability make it indispensable for climbers, cavers, sailors, and rescue personnel.

How to Tie It:

1. Begin by forming a small loop in the rope, leaving enough slack for the desired size of the knot.
2. Pass the working end of the rope through the loop from underneath, making sure the rope crosses over itself.
3. Bring the working end around the standing part of the rope, forming a loop that passes behind the standing part.
4. Pass the working end back through the original loop created in step 1, ensuring it follows the same path.
5. Pull both ends of the rope to tighten the knot securely. Ensure the knot is dressed neatly, with no twists or tangles.

FIG. 9   FIG. 10

FIGS. 9 and 10.—Figure-eight knots.

Learning and practicing these knots will make your climbing adventures way safer and more fun. It's all about getting the hang of them so you can use them easily when you're out exploring.

Mastering Rigging Knots

In outdoor activities, the ability to tie effective rigging knots is foundational for tasks such as setting up tents, constructing shelters, or building structures in bushcraft scenarios. Let's delve into a selection of key rigging knots, understanding their applications and mastering the art of secure and reliable tying.

Taut Line Hitch

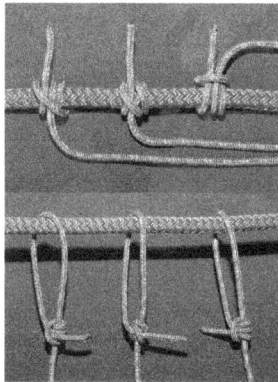

The taut line hitch is prized for its ability to create an adjustable loop that holds tension without slipping.

The taut line hitch is prized for its ability to create an adjustable loop that holds tension without slipping. Employ the taut line hitch when setting up tent guy lines or constructing shelters, allowing for easy adjustment to changing conditions.

How to Tie It:

1. Start by forming a loop in the rope, leaving enough slack for the desired size of the hitch.

2. Pass the working end of the rope around the standing part (the main length of the rope) from behind, creating a loop.

3. Bring the working end around the standing part once more, creating a second loop parallel to the first one.

4. Thread the working end through both loops from underneath, ensuring it follows the same path.

5. Pull the working end to tighten the knot securely. To adjust the tension of the line, simply slide the hitch along the standing part of the rope.

You already know about the clove hitch, which is used to secure a line to a post or a pole. You can also utilize the clove hitch when constructing outdoor structures, tying off ropes to create stable connections.

Timber Hitch

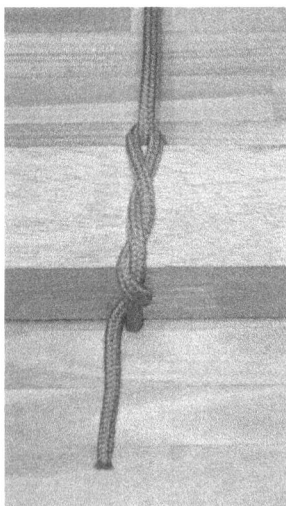

Timber hitch knot.
Attribution-ShareAlike 3.0 Unported, CC BY-SA 3.0 DEED
<https://creativecommons.org/licenses/by-sa/3.0/deed.en >
https://commons.wikimedia.org/wiki/File:Timber_Hitch_Final.jpg

The timber hitch excels at gripping round things (think trees), making it efficient for securing loads to poles or branches. Its ability to grip tightly under tension makes it a good choice for hauling and securing loads in various settings, from logging to outdoor construction projects.

How to Tie It:

1. Begin by wrapping the rope around the object you're securing, making at least two full turns.

2. After wrapping the rope, cross the working end over the standing part (the main length of the rope).

3. Bring the working end under the wraps you made around the object.

4. Pull the working end to tighten the knot securely against the object. Ensure the wraps are snug and evenly spaced.

Despite its tight grip, the Timber Hitch is relatively easy to release after bearing a load, making it convenient for temporary applications. For added security, you can tie a Half Hitch after the Timber Hitch to prevent it from slipping.

Prusik Knot

Prusik Knot.
StromBer 19:54, 22. Mär. 2008 (CET), CC BY-SA 2.0 DE
<https://creativecommons.org/licenses/by-sa/2.0/de/deed.en>, via Wikimedia Commons.
https://commons.wikimedia.org/wiki/File:PrusikNormalgeschlagen.jpg

Named after Austrian mountaineer Karl Prusik, the prusik knot is a versatile hitch that grips a rope when tensioned but slides smoothly when loosened. You can tie the prusik knot to create adjustable attachment points on climbing or rigging ropes during bushcraft activities. It's valued for its ability to grip a rope securely when tensioned, allowing climbers to ascend or descend ropes safely, as well as for various rescue scenarios.

How to Tie It:

1. Begin by forming a small loop in a piece of smaller diameter cord or rope, known as the prusik loop.

2. Pass the prusik loop around the main rope (the rope you'll be ascending or descending), ensuring it crosses over itself.

3. Wrap the prusik loop around the main rope several times, typically 3 to 5 wraps depending on the diameter of the ropes and the desired friction.

4. Pass the end of the Prusik loop through itself, creating a girth hitch around the main rope. Make sure the loop passes over the wraps you've created.

5. Pull both ends of the Prusik loop and the main rope simultaneously to tighten the knot securely.

Trucker's Hitch

Trucker's Hitch.
StromBer, CC0, via Wikimedia Commons.
https://commons.wikimedia.org/wiki/File:TruckHitch_024.jpg

The trucker's hitch is a knot that provides plenty of strong tension for holding loads on the back of the truck. Use this knot when typing down heavy outdoor structures or loads. It provides a mechanical advantage that allows you to tighten the rope securely, making it a great knot for transportation, camping, and various outdoor activities where a strong and reliable tie-down is essential.

How to Tie It:

1. Begin by forming a loop in the rope near the object you're securing. This loop will serve as the anchor point for the knot.
2. Take the working end of the rope and pass it through the loop, creating a slip knot-like configuration.
3. Pull the working end of the rope away from the anchor point and pass it around the object you're securing.
4. Bring the working end of the rope back towards the anchor point and pass it through the loop you created earlier, essentially creating a loop around the standing part of the rope.
5. Pull the working end of the rope to tighten the knot securely. This will create tension on the rope, effectively securing the load.
6. To prevent the knot from loosening, finish off with one or two half hitches around the standing part of the rope.

Mastering Essential Fishing Knots

For anglers, learning the best fishing knots is basic to the sport; those hooks and lures must stay on the line! Let's delve into key fishing knots, understand their applications, and master the art of knot tying for a successful and enjoyable fishing experience.

Palomar Knot

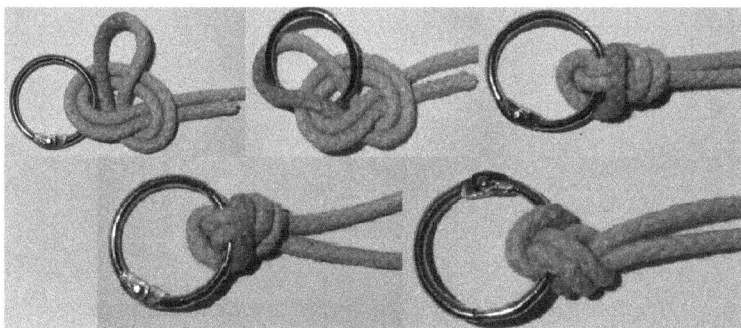

Palomar knot.

The Palomar Knot is a popular knot among anglers for its simplicity and strength. It's particularly well-suited for tying fishing line to hooks, swivels, or lures. With its reliable hold and ease of tying, the palomar Knot is a go-to choice for many fishing enthusiasts.

How to Tie It:

1. Double the fishing line and pass it through the eye of the hook, swivel, or lure, creating a loop.
2. Tie a simple overhand knot with the doubled line, leaving a loop large enough to pass the hook, swivel, or lure through.
3. Pass the hook, swivel, or lure through the loop created by the overhand knot.
4. Moisten the knot with water or saliva to reduce friction, then pull both ends of the line to tighten the knot securely against the eye of the hook, swivel, or lure.
5. Trim any excess line extending beyond the knot, leaving a small tag end for added security.
6. Always inspect the palomar Knot after tying to ensure it's tightened securely and there are no signs of slippage or weakness.

Improved Clinch Knot

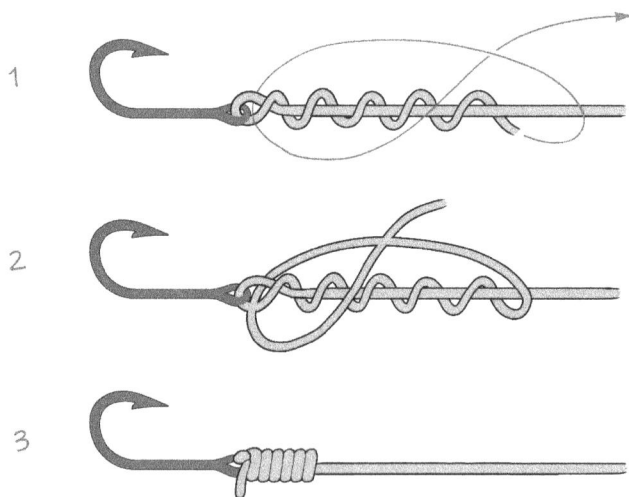

The Improved Clinch Knot

The Improved Clinch Knot is a classic knot used by anglers to tie fishing lines to hooks, lures, or swivels. It's known for its reliability, strength, and ease of tying, making it a favorite among fishermen of all skill levels.

How to Tie It:

1. Pass the end of the fishing line through the eye of the hook or lure, ensuring you leave enough line to work with.

2. Take the tag end (the loose end of the line) and wrap it around the standing line (the main line) at least five or six times. Ensure the wraps are neat and tightly wound.

3. After completing the wraps, thread the tag end through the loop formed between the eye of the hook and the wraps. This creates a new loop near the eye of the hook.

4. Pass the tag end through the loop you just created. This will form a second loop around the standing line.

5. Moisten the knot with water or saliva to reduce friction, then pull both the tag end and the standing line simultaneously to tighten the knot securely against the eye of the hook or lure.

6. Trim any excess tag end extending beyond the knot, leaving a small tag for added security.

Uni-Knot (Duncan Loop)

Uni-knot.
StromBer 11:52, 31. Mär. 2008 (CEST), CC BY-SA 2.0 DE
<*https://creativecommons.org/licenses/by-sa/2.0/de/deed.en*>, *via Wikimedia Commons:*
https://commons.wikimedia.org/wiki/File:Arborknoten2.JPG

The uni-knot, also known as the Duncan loop, offers strength and versatility, making it suitable for various fishing applications. Use the uni-knot for connecting hooks, swivels, or lures to your fishing line, providing a robust and adaptable knot.

How to Tie It:

1. Pass the end of the fishing line through the eye of the hook or lure, leaving a few inches of tag end to work with.

2. Form a small loop by doubling back the tag end of the line parallel to the standing line (the main line).

3. Take the tag end and wrap it around both the doubled line and the standing line, making at least 4 to 6 wraps. Ensure the wraps are neat and tightly wound.

4. After completing the wraps, pass the tag end back through the loop you created in step 2, entering from the same side as the original tag end.

5. Moisten the knot with water or saliva to reduce friction, then pull both the tag end and the standing line simultaneously to tighten the knot securely against the eye of the hook or lure.

6. Trim any excess tag end extending beyond the knot, leaving a small tag for added security.

Surgeon's Knot

Surgeon's knot.
Attribution-ShareAlike 3.0 Unported, CC BY-SA 3.0 DEED
<https://creativecommons.org/licenses/by-sa/3.0/deed.en >
https://commons.wikimedia.org/wiki/File:Surgeon%27s_knot.jpg

The surgeon's knot excels at joining two lines together. Anglers often use it to tie leader material to fishing line or to attach two pieces of fishing line together. Use it when attaching leaders, adding to your fishing line, or creating strong connections between lines of different diameters.

How to Tie It:

1. Lay the ends of the two lines parallel to each other, overlapping by a few inches.

2. Tie a simple overhand knot by passing one end of the line over the other and then threading it back through the loop created.

3. Pass the same end of the line through the loop again, creating a double overhand knot. Do not tighten it completely yet.

4. Repeat steps 2 and 3 with the end of the other line, tying another double overhand knot around the standing part of the first line.

5. Moisten the knots with saliva or water to lubricate them, then pull both ends of the lines simultaneously to tighten the knots securely together. Ensure both knots snug up against each other.

6. Trim any excess tag ends close to the knots, leaving a small tag for added security.

Blood Knot

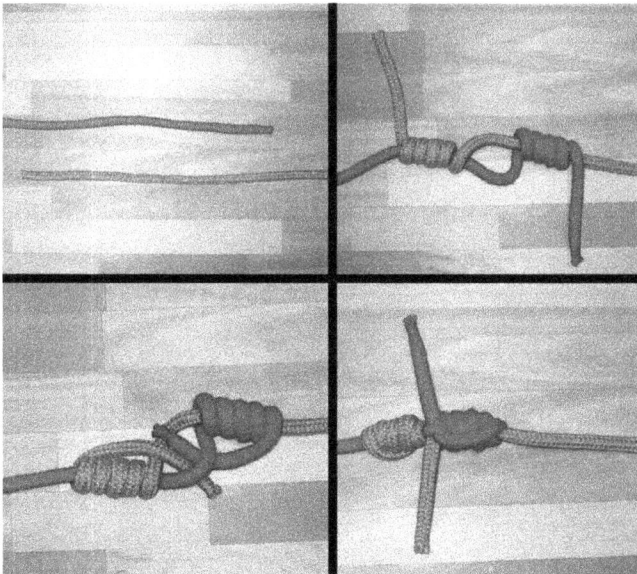

Blood knot.

The blood knot is ideal for seamlessly joining two lines of similar diameter, maintaining strength and integrity. Use the blood knot when creating leaders or connecting sections of fishing lines.

How to Tie It:

1. Lay the ends of the two lines parallel to each other, overlapping by several inches.

2. Tie a simple overhand knot by passing one end of the line over the other and then threading it back through the loop created. Do not tighten it completely yet.

3. Starting with one end, wrap it around the standing part of the other line, making at least five wraps. Ensure the wraps are neat and tightly wound.

4. Repeat step 3 with the other end of the line, wrapping it around the standing part of the first line in the opposite direction.

5. After completing the wraps with both ends, pass each end through the middle of the wraps, entering from opposite directions.

6. Moisten the knots with saliva or water to lubricate them, then pull both ends of the lines simultaneously to tighten the knots securely together. Ensure both knots snug up against each other.

7. Trim any excess tag ends close to the knots, leaving a small tag for added security.

Arbor Knot

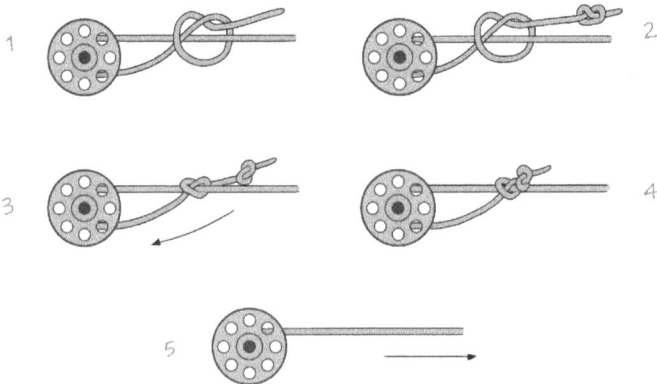

Arbor knot

The arbor knot is designed for securing a fishing line to the reel, ensuring a reliable connection between your line and the spool. Use this knot when spooling a new line onto your fishing reel; you'll have a secure attachment and get great performance from your reel.

How to Tie:

1. Pass the line through the arbor.

2. Tie a simple overhand knot around the line.

3. Wrap the free end around the arbor and standing line.

4. Pass the free end through the overhand knot.

5. Moisten and tighten the knot.

6. Trim excess line.

Loop Knot (Non-Slip Loop Knot)

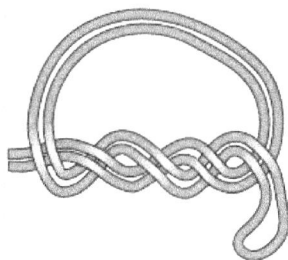

Surgeon's Loop Knot

Loop Knot.

https://commons.wikimedia.org/wiki/File:Surgeon%27s_Loop_knot.svg

The loop knot (or non-slip loop knot) enhances lure action by allowing them to move more freely, making it suitable for certain types of lures. Use the loop knot when attaching lures that are designed for increased movement and action in the water.

How to Tie:

1. Form a small loop at the end of the line.
2. Pass the tag end through the loop, then wrap it around the standing line.
3. Pass the tag end back through the loop.
4. Moisten and tighten the knot.

Building Outdoor Structures

Knowing how to build things is super cool when you're on an adventure outside! Learning special knots and ways to tie ropes together is like unlocking a secret power to make strong, awesome stuff outdoors. Here are some key knots that are great for building:

Japanese Square Lashing: This knot is super strong and perfect for making parts of your outdoor fort or anything else stick together really well.

How to Tie:

1. Position two poles at a right angle.
2. Wrap the rope around both poles near the intersection.
3. Make a clove hitch around the vertical pole.
4. Wrap the rope tightly around both poles, making 5-7 wraps.
5. Tie two half hitches around the vertical pole.
6. Tuck the tail under a wrap to finish.
7. Trim excess rope if needed.

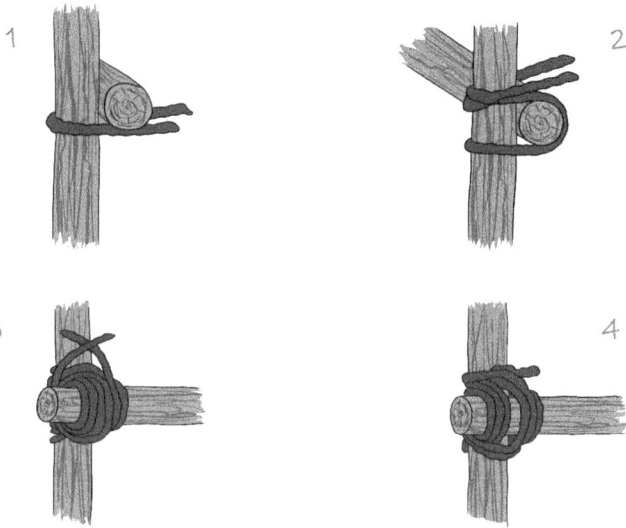

Japanese Square Lashing.

Shear Lashing: This knot keeps things standing if you're building something that might get pushed from the sides.

How To Tie:

1. Position two poles parallel to each other.
2. Place the rope over both poles, leaving a tail hanging.
3. Wrap the rope tightly around both poles, making multiple wraps.
4. Cross the rope between the poles.
5. Wrap the rope around both poles again, going in the opposite direction.
6. Tie two half hitches around one of the poles.
7. Tuck the tail under a wrap to finish.
8. Trim excess rope if needed.

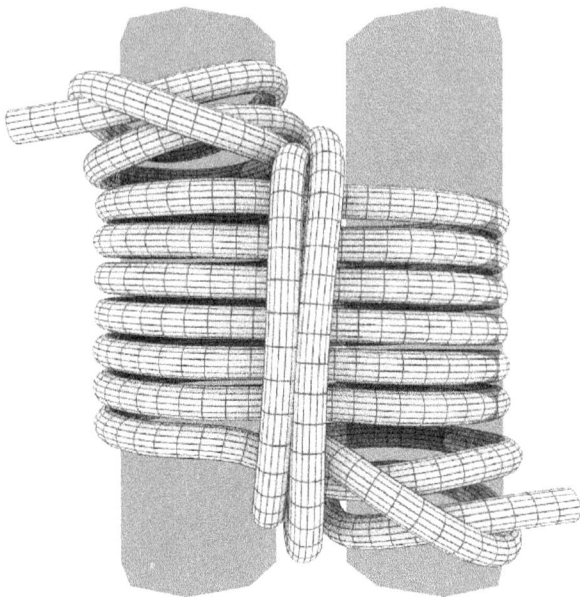

Shear Lashing.

Taut-Line Hitch: This adjustable knot is awesome for making tent lines tighter or looser without a fuss.

How to Tie:

1. Wrap the rope around a fixed object, forming a loop.
2. Pass the free end of the rope through the loop.
3. Wrap the free end around the standing part of the rope.
4. Pass the free end through the loop again, forming a second loop.
5. Tighten the knot by pulling the free end while holding the standing part.
6. Adjust the tension by sliding the knot along the standing part.

Alpine Butterfly Knot: Need a loop in the middle of your rope? This knot's got you covered. It's great for hanging things up or tying stuff down.

1. Form a loop in the rope, crossing one end over the standing part.
2. Bring the end back underneath the standing part, forming a second loop.
3. Cross the end over the first loop and tuck it under the second loop.
4. Pull the ends to tighten the knot, forming the Alpine Butterfly.

Alpine butterfly knot.

Practicing these knots means you can make all sorts of cool constructions that hold up when you're exploring the great outdoors. Imagine the amazing camps and shelters you can build!

Survival Knots for the Wild

Being quick and smart with knots can save the day in the wild. Here are some super important knots for survival:

Tourniquet Knot: If someone's hurt and bleeding a lot, this knot can help stop the bleeding until you get help.

1. Wrap a piece of fabric or bandage tightly around the limb above the wound.

2. Tie a half knot with the ends of the fabric, making sure it's snug against the limb.

3. Tie a second half knot on top of the first one, securing the tourniquet in place.

4. Twist a stick or rod into the knot to tighten further if necessary.

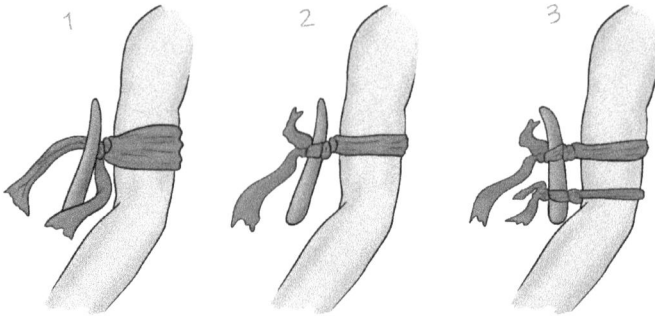

A Tourniquet Knot.

Tripod Lashing: With three sticks and this knot, you can make a sturdy stand for shelters or to hang things up high.

1. Lay three poles parallel to each other, forming a tripod.
2. Tie a clove hitch around one of the poles near the top.
3. Wrap the rope tightly around all three poles, making multiple wraps.
4. Finish with two half hitches around one of the poles.
5. Tuck the tail under a wrap to secure.
6. Adjust the tension and position of the lashing as needed.

Fireman's Chair Knot: Need to lift or lower someone in an emergency? This knot makes it possible.

1. Tie a Figure-8 Knot on a bight in the rope to create a loop.
2. Pass the loop around the person's waist to form a harness.
3. Optionally, create leg loops for stability.
4. Tie a second Figure-8 Knot on a bight as a backup.
5. Attach the rope to the harness using a carabiner or secure knot.
6. Lower the person using a belay device or friction knot.
7. Maintain clear communication throughout the process.
8. Perform safety checks on all equipment and knots before lowering.

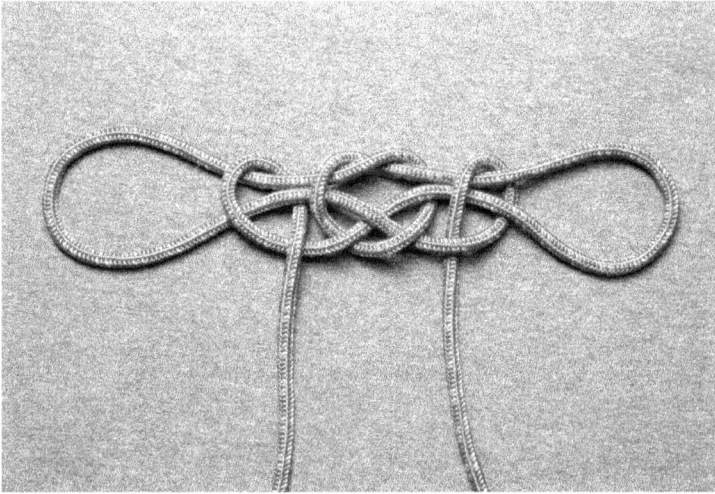

Fireman's Chair Knot.

Clove Hitch: Fast and easy, this knot lets you tie a rope to a pole or tree super quick, perfect for making shelters or other handy survival tools.

1. Pass the end of the rope around the object you're tying to.

2. Cross the end over the standing part of the rope to form an X.

3. Cross the end under the standing part of the rope, creating a loop.

4. Pass the end over the object and through the loop.

5. Tighten the knot by pulling both ends of the rope.

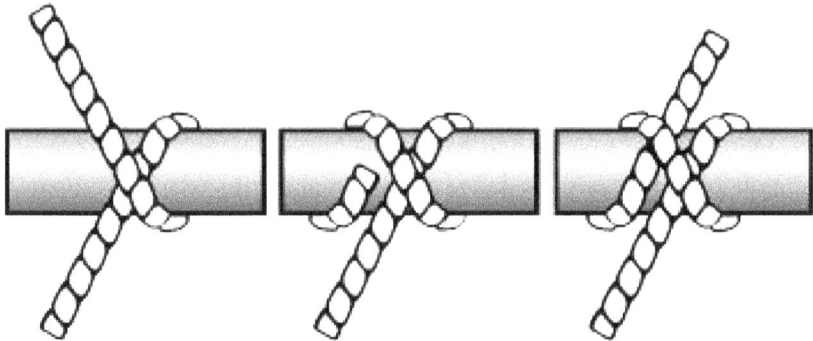

Clove Hitch.

Knowing these knots gives you the skills to handle tough spots in nature. Keep practicing, and you'll be ready for anything the wild throws at you.

Section 6: Everyday Knots

Knot tying is a super cool skill that you can use in lots of ways every day! It's perfect for ensuring your tent stays put, building shelters, and keeping your gear safe when camping, hiking, or sailing.

At home, you can use simple knots for things like tying up packages, keeping your shoes on your feet, or keeping your toys and stuff neat and tidy. Knots are also important for people who sail boats, go fishing, or build things because they help make everything safe and work better.

In emergencies, like when someone needs to be rescued, knowing the right knots can be super important. Learning to tie knots can make you better at solving problems, help you do things on your own, and give you handy skills for all kinds of situations.

Single Shoelace Knot

The single shoelace knot, often called the "bunny ears" method, is simple to do! You probably already know this one: start by crossing one shoelace over the other, creating a simple X shape. Then, take one end and pass it under the other lace, pulling it through the loop created. Tighten the knot by pulling both ends at the same time.

Practical Applications

The single shoelace knot is a quick and efficient way to secure footwear. You'll use this every time you put on your sneakers and in many other places around home and school. Look around - you'll see it everywhere!

Double Shoelace Knot

Building on the single knot, the double shoelace knot adds an extra layer of security. After creating the initial knot, repeat the process by crossing one lace over the other and pulling it through the loop again. This creates a double loop, so your knot is extra strong!

Practical Applications

The double shoelace knot is particularly useful in situations where shoes may undergo a lot of action, like sports or P.E. This knot doesn't come loose easily, so you won't have to worry about tripping all over the place!

Everyday Tasks

Knot tying extends beyond shoelaces and finds application in various everyday tasks. For instance, securing bags of snacks with a knot helps preserve freshness, while bundling items together using a knot helps when you're trying to store things.

School and Work

Knots come in handy for securing backpacks or luggage and organizing materials. Students use knots to fasten art supplies, and professionals might use them to bundle cables or secure items during transit.

Recreational Activities

Knot tying is essential during recreational activities such as camping, hiking, and fishing. Whether setting up a tent, securing gear, or even improvising solutions on the spot, the ability to tie different knots becomes very important in the outdoors!

Universal Tools in Daily Life

Single and double shoelace knots are used a lot in our daily lives. Look around: you'll find these knots keeping shoes on tightly and helping keep things organized neatly.

Fisherman's Loop

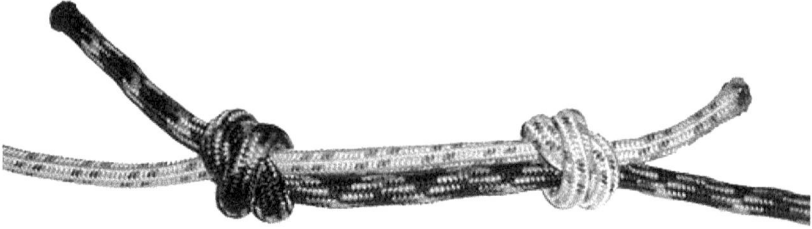

The Fisherman's Loop, also called the *Angler's Loop*, is a handy fishing knot. It makes a strong loop at the end of your line so you can quickly hook on your bait or other gear. Fishermen love it because it never lets them down.

How to Tie the Fisherman's Loop:

1. Start with a basic loop knot in your line.
2. Thread the loose end (that's the tag end) through the loop two times.
3. Wet the knot a bit to make tightening easier.
4. Pull on both the main line and the tag end together to snug it up tight.

Why It's Awesome:

It's perfect for tying on all your fishing stuff securely. It works great for different kinds of fishing, whether in a lake or the ocean.

Not Just for Fishing:

- Use it to make a quick handle on bags or tie things down tightly.
- Great for camping or outdoor stuff when you need a loop that you can trust.

Super Strong Knot:

The Fisherman's Loop keeps most of the line's strength, even under lots of pressure. That means your loop stays tight, even when you've got a big fish on the line!

Bow Tie Knot

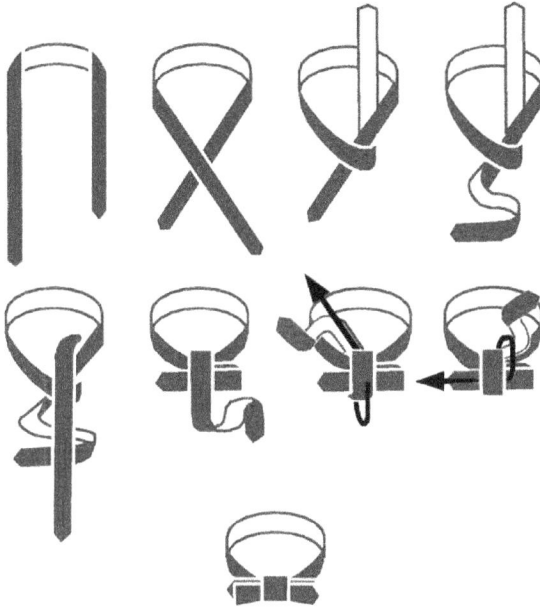

The bow tie knot is a classic and elegant method of tying a necktie.

The bow tie knot (also known as the butterfly knot) is a classic and elegant method of tying a necktie. This knot resembles the shape of a bow tie; hence, its name. It is commonly used in formal and semi-formal settings, adding a touch of sophistication to one's attire.

Tying the Bow Tie Knot

1. Begin with the wide end of the tie on your right side and the narrow end on your left.

2. Cross the wide end over the narrow end.

3. Bring the wide end around and behind the narrow end, creating a loop.

4. Pull the wide end up and through the loop.

5. Tighten the knot by adjusting the ends and the bow's size.

Practical Applications

The bow tie knot is primarily used with neckties, especially when aiming for a refined and stylish appearance. It is often chosen for formal events, weddings, or any occasion with a desired touch of elegance.

Alternatives to the Bow Tie Knot

While the bow tie knot is a classic choice for formal occasions, various alternative knots offer versatility and cater to different collar types, tie widths, and personal styles. Experimenting with different knots allows individuals to express their fashion preferences and adapt their necktie choices to various settings.

Four-in-Hand Knot

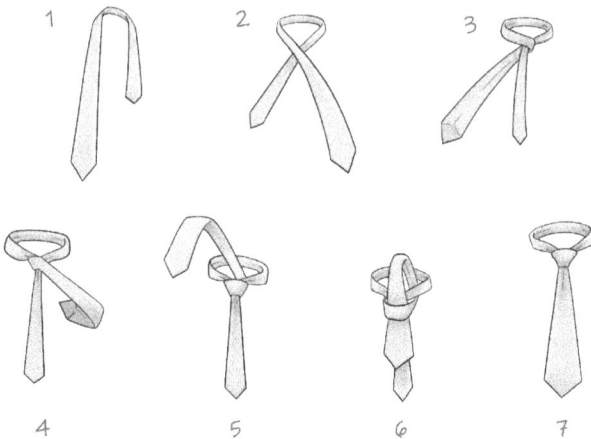

Four-in-Hand Knot.

The Four-in-Hand Knot is one of the most classic and widely used necktie knots. It's known for its simplicity, versatility, and slightly asymmetric appearance. Named after the carriage drivers of the 19th century who tied their scarves with this knot, the Four-in-Hand is suitable for most occasions, from casual to business settings.

How to Tie It:

1. Start by draping the tie around your neck with the wide end on your right side and the narrow end on your left side. Adjust the length so that the wide end is longer than the narrow end.

2. Cross the wide end of the tie over the narrow end, forming an "X" at the front of your neck.

3. Bring the wide end underneath the narrow end, passing it from right to left.

4. Bring the wide end up through the loop around your neck, passing it from underneath to create a diagonal loop on the right side.

5. Bring the wide end across the front of the knot, passing it from right to left.

6. Bring the wide end up through the loop at the front of the knot, passing it from underneath to create a second diagonal loop on the left side.

7. Hold onto the narrow end with one hand and use the other hand to slide the knot up towards your neck, adjusting the tightness and symmetry as desired.

8. Once the knot is tightened to your liking, adjust the collar and the front of the tie to ensure a neat and stylish appearance.

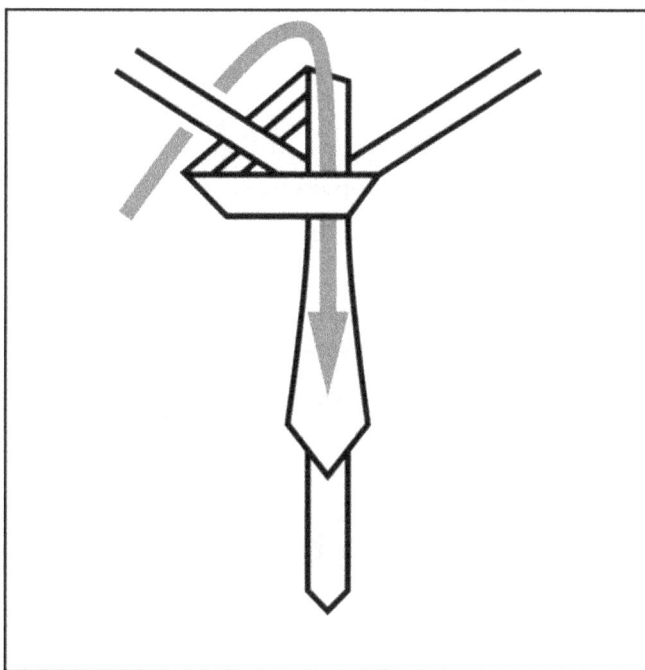

Four-in-Hand knot works great for most ties and looks a bit off-center.

Windsor Knot

Big and shaped like a triangle, this knot fits shirts with wide collars and is awesome for thick ties.

How to Tie It:

1. Start by draping the tie around your neck with the wide end on your right side and the narrow end on your left side. Adjust the length so that the wide end is longer than the narrow end.

2. Cross the wide end of the tie over the narrow end, forming an X at the front of your neck.

3. Bring the wide end underneath the narrow end, passing it from right to left.

4. Now bring the wide end up through the loop around your neck, passing it from underneath to create a diagonal loop on the right side.

5. Bring the wide end across the front of the knot, passing it from left to right.

6. Bring the wide end up through the loop at the front of the knot, passing it from underneath to create a second diagonal loop on the left side.

7. Pass the wide end down through the loop at the front of the knot, creating a third diagonal loop on the right side.

8. Bring the wide end across the front of the knot once more, passing it from right to left.

9. Pass the wide end up through the loop at the front of the knot, creating a fourth diagonal loop on the left side.

10. Hold onto the narrow end with one hand and use the other hand to slide the knot up towards your neck, adjusting the tightness and symmetry as desired.

11. Once the knot is tightened to your liking, adjust the collar and the front of the tie to ensure a neat and symmetrical appearance.

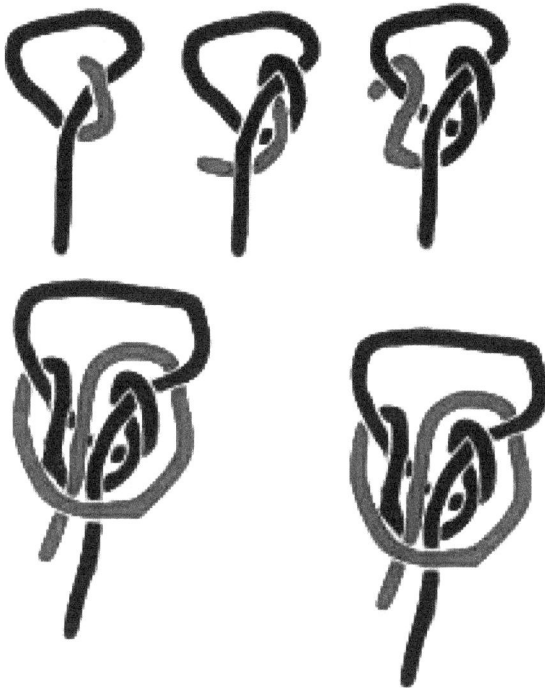

Windsor knot fits shirts with wide collars and is awesome for thick ties.

Fúlvio, CC BY-SA 3.0 <https://creativecommons.org/licenses/by-sa/3.0>, via Wikimedia Commons: https://commons.wikimedia.org/wiki/File:Double_windsor.svg

Half-Windsor Knot

It's not as big as the Windsor, but it's still great for all kinds of events. It goes well with medium-size ties.

How to Tie It:

1. Start by draping the tie around your neck with the wide end on your right side and the narrow end on your left side.

2. Cross the wide end of the tie over the narrow end, forming an X.

3. Bring the wide end underneath the narrow end, passing it from right to left and then across the front of the knot, passing it from left to right.

4. Bring the wide end up through the loop around your neck, passing it from underneath to create a diagonal loop on the right side.

5. Bring the wide end across the front of the knot once more, passing it from right to left.

6. Bring the wide end up through the loop at the front of the knot, passing it from underneath to create a second diagonal loop on the left side.

7. Pass the wide end down through the loop at the front of the knot, creating a third diagonal loop on the right side.

8. Hold onto the narrow end with one hand and use the other hand to slide the knot up towards your neck.

9. Adjust the collar and the front of the tie to ensure a neat appearance.

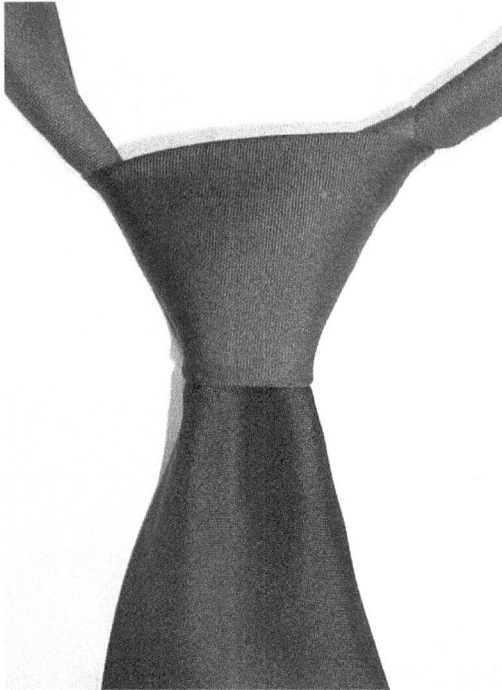

Half-Windsor knot.

Pratt (Shelby) Knot

Kind of like the Four-in-Hand but tidier and a bit bigger. It's good for just about any tie.

How to Tie It:

1. Start by draping the tie around your neck similar to the above mentioned styles and cross it to form an X.

2. Bring the wide end underneath the narrow end, passing it from right to left.

3. Now bring the wide end up through the loop around your neck, passing it from underneath to create a diagonal loop on the left side.

4. Bring the wide end across the front of the knot, passing it from left to right and up through the loop at the front of the knot, passing it from underneath to create a second diagonal loop on the right side.

5. Create a third diagonal loop on the left side.

6. Adjust the tightness and symmetry as desired.

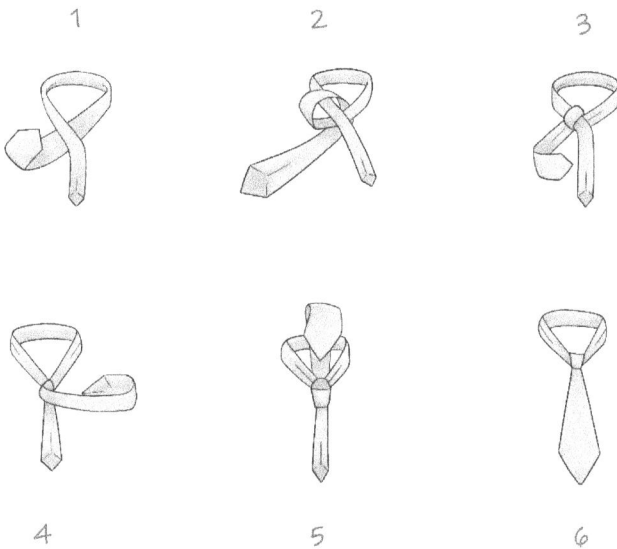

This knot is good for just about any tie.

Eldredge Knot

Named after its creator, Jeffrey Eldredge, this knot is not for the faint of heart but is sure to make a bold statement when worn. While it may take some practice to master, the Eldredge Knot offers a unique and stylish option for those looking to stand out with their neckwear.

How to Tie It:

1. Start by draping like you did in the previous knots.

2. Make an X by crossing the wide end of the tie over the narrow end.

3. Bring the wide end up through the loop around your neck, passing it from underneath to create a diagonal loop on the left side.

4. Bring the wide end across the front of the knot, passing it from left to right.

5. Bring the wide end up through the loop at the front of the knot, passing it from underneath to create a second diagonal loop on the right side.

6. Pass the wide end down through the lower diagonal loop on the right side of the knot.

7. Pass the wide end up through the upper diagonal loop on the right side of the knot.

8. Bring the wide end across the front of the knot once more, passing it from right to left.

9. Pass the wide end down through the loop at the front of the knot, creating a third diagonal loop on the left side.

10. Once the knot is tightened, adjust for a neat look.

Eldredge knot.

Trinity Knot

The Trinity Knot, also known as the Triquetra Knot, is a stylish and intricate necktie knot that resembles a three-pointed Celtic symbol. It's a less common knot choice but offers a unique and eye-catching appearance that is sure to draw attention.

How to Tie It:

1. Drape the tie around your neck and cross it, forming an X at the front of your neck.

2. Bring the wide end up through the loop around your neck, passing it from underneath to create a diagonal loop on the left side.

3. Bring the wide end across the front of the knot, passing it from left to right.

4. Bring the wide end up through the loop at the front of the knot, passing it from underneath to create a second diagonal loop on the right side.

5. Pass the wide end down through the lower diagonal loop on the right side of the knot.

6. Pass the wide end up through the upper diagonal loop on the right side of the knot.

Kelvin Knot

The Kelvin Knot is a lesser-known necktie knot that offers a unique and asymmetrical appearance. Named after the physicist Lord Kelvin, this knot features a distinctive diagonal knot structure that adds an interesting flair to your neckwear. While not as common as some other knots, the Kelvin Knot is a stylish option for those looking to stand out with their tie choice. Here's how to tie it:

How to Tie It:

1. Drape the tie and form an X by crossing the two ends like you did earlier.

2. Bring the wide end underneath the narrow end, passing it to the left side.

3. Bring the wide end up through the loop around your neck, creating a diagonal loop on the left side of the knot.

4. Bring the wide end across the front of the knot, passing it from left to right.

5. Pass the wide end down through the loop at the front of the knot, forming a second diagonal loop on the right side.

6. Adjust for a neat look.

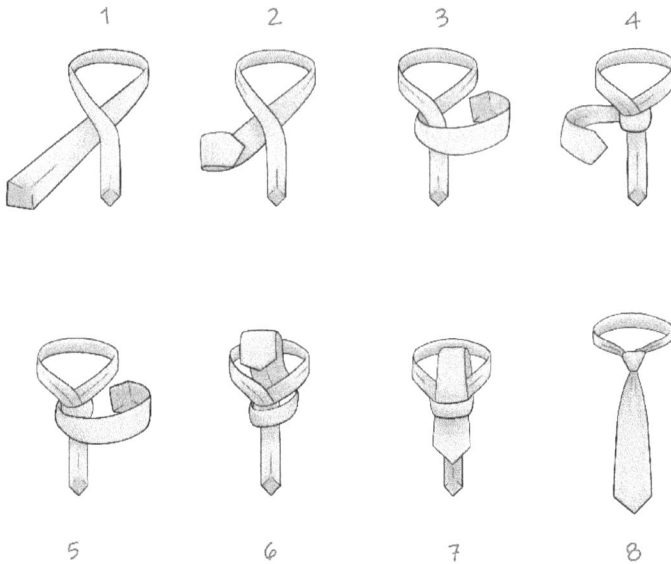

A smaller, easy knot that's perfect for everyday wear and goes well with thin collars and lighter ties.

Oriental Knot

The oriental knot, also known as the simple knot or kent knot, is a classic and elegant necktie knot that is simple to tie and well-suited for thin or wide ties. It has a symmetrical and streamlined appearance, making it a popular choice for both formal and casual occasions.

How to Tie It:

1. Drape the tie around your neck and form a cross.

2. Bring the wide end underneath the narrow end, wrapping it around the narrow end from right to left.

3. Bring the wide end up through the loop around your neck, creating a simple knot.

4. Pass the wide end down through the loop at the front of the knot, tightening it slightly.

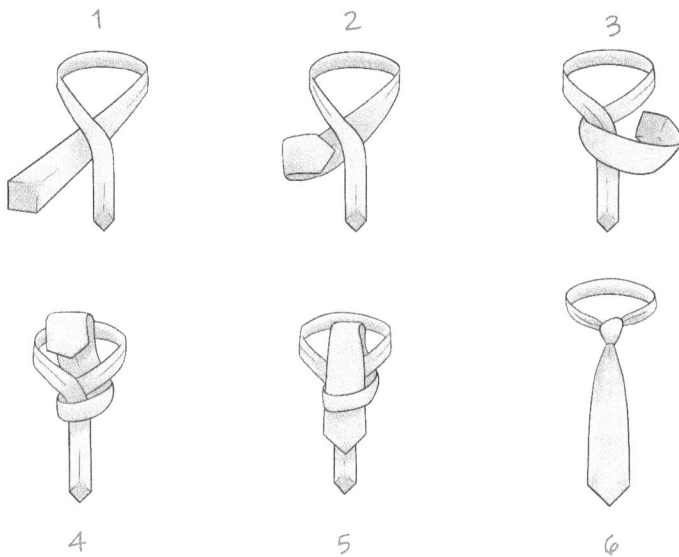

A super simple, tiny knot that's quick to tie

The Cool Parcel Bend Knot

The Parcel Bend Knot.
Cobanyastigi, CC0, via Wikimedia Commons:
https://commons.wikimedia.org/wiki/File:KolanBagi%C3%96n.jpg

The Parcel Bend Knot, also known as the Harness Bend, is a super-strong knot that's perfect for tying together two ropes, even if they're different sizes. It makes sure they stay tightly connected, which is awesome for when you need a really secure tie.

How to Tie It:

1. Place the big rope next to the smaller one so they overlap a bit.
2. Wrap the skinny rope around both ropes a few times.
3. Tuck the end of the skinny rope under and pull it through the loop you made.
4. Pull on both ends of the skinny rope to tighten the knot.

Where to Use It:

- Camping adventures
- Sailing the seas
- Building cool stuff
- Anytime you need to tie ropes together tightly

This knot is great because it won't slip, even if you pull really hard, making it perfect for all kinds of fun activities and important tasks. Whether you're making something or need a quick fix, the Parcel Bend Knot has got your back!

Section 7: Knotting for Fun

Tying knots can help you relax and feel less stressed. It's like doing a calming activity that lets your mind focus on one thing; repetitive and rhythmic; this is like a simple and slow dance for your hands. Doing this can make your mind forget about worries and be present in the moment. It's like a break from the business of the day. Feeling the texture of the rope in your hands is nice, and it's like a little fun challenge to create different knots. Tying knots is not just about making things; it's about taking a quiet moment for yourself, feeling good when you finish, and letting your mind relax. It's like a simple, hands-on way to feel calm and accomplished.

Decorative Knots

Crafting and jewelry-making offer wonderful opportunities to showcase visually appealing, decorative knots. Here are some knots that can add flair to your creations:

Celtic Knot

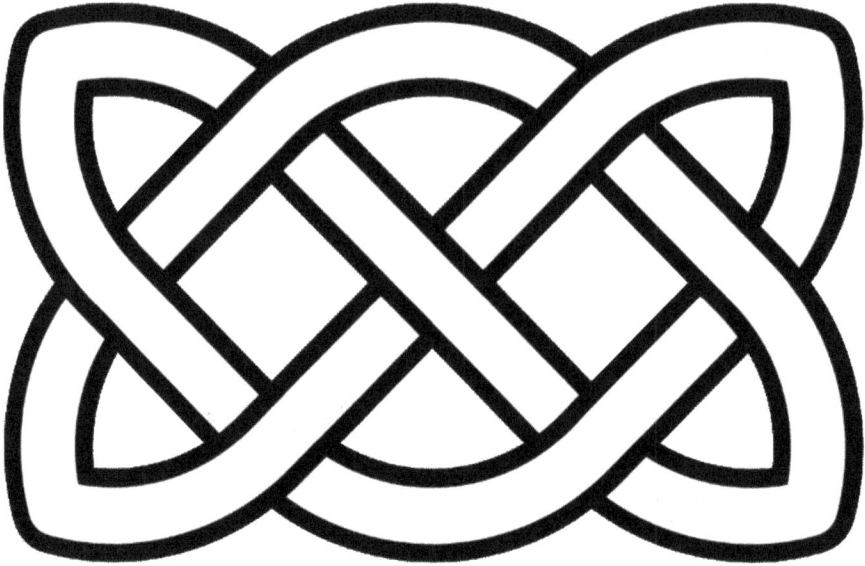

Celtic knot.

The Celtic knot is a symbol of eternity, and its intricate design is visually captivating. This knot involves weaving a continuous cord into a mesmerizing pattern. It's often used in jewelry, especially as pendants or focal points in bracelets.

Instructions:

1. Hold one end of the string in each hand.
2. Cross the right end of the string over the left to make a loop on the left side.
3. Wrap the right end behind the left end and pull it through the loop.
4. Pull both ends to slightly tighten the knot.
5. Repeat steps two to four using the left end of the string.
6. Pull both ends to tighten the knot.

Monkey's Fist

Monkey's fist knot.

No machine-readable author provided. Tortillovsky assumed (based on copyright claims)., CC BY-SA 3.0 <http://creativecommons.org/licenses/by-sa/3.0/>, via Wikimedia Commons: https://commons.wikimedia.org/wiki/File:Knot_Monkey_Fist.jpg

Instructions:

1. Hold the end of the string in your hand and wrap it around your fingers to create a loop.

2. Gently slide the loop off your fingers and hold it between your thumb and index finger.

3. Wrap the string around the loop. Make sure to go in the opposite direction than the one you used to make the first loop. Do this until you have three layers of wraps.

4. Pull the end of the string through the center of the wraps until the knot is tight.

The Monkey's Fist knot is a round, ball-like knot that adds a nautical and decorative touch. It's often used in keychains or as a focal point in necklaces. Vary the size and experiment with different materials for diverse looks.

Chinese Button Knot

The Chinese Button knot is an ornamental knot that resembles a flower. It works well as a decorative closure for bracelets or necklaces, adding a touch of elegance. Play with different thread or cord colors to create a vibrant bloom.

Instructions:

1. Fold the string in half, find its middle point and hold it with one hand.
2. Make a loop with one end of the string and cross it over the other end.
3. Bring the bottom end up through the loop to create a new loop.
4. Pass the end through the new loop, making sure it goes under the first loop.
5. Pull the end through to tighten the knot, forming a button-like shape.

Lover's Knot (Josephine Knot)

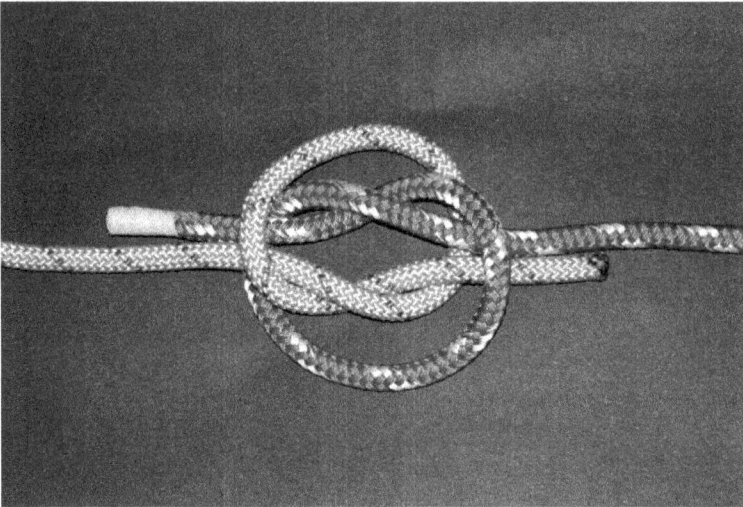

Lover's knot.

Frank van Mierlo, Attribution, via Wikimedia Commons:
https://commons.wikimedia.org/wiki/File:True_Lover%27s_knot-0.jpg

Instructions:

1. Hold both ends of the string and tie a simple knot, leaving a loop at the top.
2. Take the left end of the string and make a loop toward the right.
3. Take the right end of the string and make a loop toward the left, then pass the right loop under the left loop.
4. Pass the right string over the left loop and through the right loop, it should look like a pretzel.
5. Pull both ends of the string to tighten the knot.

The Lover's knot is a delicate and romantic knot that creates an intertwined pattern. It's popular in wedding-themed jewelry or as a focal point in elegant accessories like headbands or earrings.

Snake Knot

The Snake knot, resembling the body of a snake, is both visually interesting and versatile. Use it to create bracelets or anklets with a unique and textured design. Experiment with multiple colors for a striking effect.

Instructions:

1. Fold the string in half to find the middle point, make sure to hold this point with one hand.
2. With your other hand, make a loop with one end of the string and cross it over to the other end of your string.
3. Pull the bottom end through a loop to create a new loop and pull the end through to tighten the knot.
4. Repeat steps two to four until you reach the desired length.

Double Coin Knot

Double coin knot.

ClemRutter, CC BY-SA 4.0 <https://creativecommons.org/licenses/by-sa/4.0>, via Wikimedia Commons: https://commons.wikimedia.org/wiki/File:Double_coin_knot_3806.jpg

The Double Coin knot is a round, flat knot that adds a decorative element to accessories. It's ideal for making earrings, pendants, or even embellishments for bags. Vary the size and color to suit your design.

Instructions:
1. Make a loop to the right, then pass one of the end over it without passing it through.
2. Make another loop on the side opposite to the first one.
3. Pass the end under the loops, then over, and then under again. Pull both ends to tighten your knot.

Infinity Knot

Symbolizing eternity, the Infinity knot is a simple yet elegant choice. Incorporate it into necklaces or bracelets to add a touch of symbolism to your jewelry designs.

Diamond Knot (Lanyard Knot)

Lanyard knot.

David J. Fred, CC BY-SA 2.5 <https://creativecommons.org/licenses/by-sa/2.5>, via Wikimedia Commons: https://commons.wikimedia.org/wiki/File:Knife-lanyard-knot-ABOK-787-Final.jpg

The Diamond knot, often used in lanyards, has a distinctive diamond shape. It can either be incorporated into keychains or used as a decorative element in various crafts.

Instructions:

1. Loop a piece of your rope other the three middle fingers on your left hand. Make sure to lay the ends across your palms.
2. Make a loop with the cord on the right.
3. Flip the knot.
4. Loop the bottom cord behind the tail of the top cord.
5. Loop it over the top cord, under the middle, and over the bottom.
6. Center the knot on your palm. It should look similar to a Celtic knot.
7. Pull the top cord towards your thumb and pull it underneath the knot, leaving a little bit of space. Repeat this step with the bottom cord.
8. Pull each of the cords slowly until the knot is tight.

Experimenting with these decorative knots opens up a world of creative possibilities in crafting and jewelry making. Combine different knots and varying materials, and play with colors to express your unique style and create visually stunning pieces.

Creating Friendship Bracelets

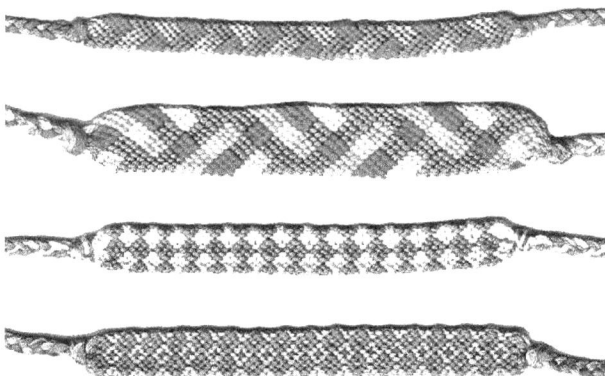

Creating friendship bracelets is a fun and creative way to express your personal style.
Raïke (see also: de:Benutzer:Raïke), CC BY-SA 3.0 <http://creativecommons.org/licenses/by-sa/3.0/>, via Wikimedia Commons:
https://commons.wikimedia.org/wiki/File:Friendship_Bracelet_square_forms.jpg

Creating friendship bracelets is a fun and creative way to express your personal style and share handmade gifts with friends. Below are step-by-step instructions for a simple diagonal stripe pattern using knotting techniques. Feel free to experiment with color choices to make your bracelet unique.

Materials Needed

- Embroidery floss (choose multiple colors)
- Scissors
- Tape or a safety pin (to secure the bracelet)

Step 1: Gather Materials

Gather your embroidery floss in the desired colors. You can choose as many colors as you like, but for simplicity, let's start with three different colors.

Step 2: Cut the Floss

Cut each color into strands, each about 24 inches long. You'll need two strands of each color. Adjust the length based on your wrist size and the desired length of the bracelet, leaving a little extra for tying knots.

Step 3: Arrange the Colors

Line up the strands side by side, making sure the colors are in the order you want for your bracelet.

Step 4: Secure with Tape or a Safety Pin

Secure one end of the strands with tape or a safety pin. This will make the braiding process easier.

Step 5: Begin Knotting

Start by taking the leftmost strand and making a "4" shape over the next strand (middle strand).

Step 6: Make a Knot

Wrap the leftmost strand behind the middle strand, pulling the end through the loop created by the "4." Pull tight to create a knot.

Step 7: Repeat with the Right Strand

Repeat the process with the rightmost strand. Make a backward "4" over the middle strand, wrap it behind, and pull through the loop.

Step 8: Continue Braiding

Continue alternating between left and right, creating a series of knots. As you progress, you'll see diagonal stripes forming.

Step 9: Add More Colors

If you want to add more colors, simply introduce new strands and continue the knotting pattern.

Step 10: Secure the End

Once your bracelet reaches the desired length, secure the end with a knot. Trim any excess floss.

Step 11: Tie the Bracelet

Tie the bracelet around your wrist, making a double knot to secure it. Trim any remaining excess floss.

Experiment with Patterns

Feel free to experiment with different patterns, such as chevrons, diamonds, or even letters. You can also add beads for extra flair. The key is to have fun and let your creativity shine through in your friendship bracelet designs.

Customize Your Gear

Creating keychains, lanyards, and zipper pulls by using knots is a fantastic and engaging craft activity for children. Not only does it foster creativity, but it also allows kids to personalize and showcase their unique style. Below are step-by-step instructions for making these items by using simple knotting techniques.

Materials Needed

- Assorted colors of paracord or lanyard cord
- Scissors
- Keyrings or clasps (for keychains)
- Swivel clasps (for lanyards)
- Small zipper pulls or clips (for zipper pulls)

Keychain

When the braid is reaches 24-30" in length, do a square weave.

Bring around the first end and do a square braid around it.

Keep doing a square braid for about 1 inch.

The finished product... before the ends are cut

Pull on the end to tighten the lanyard.

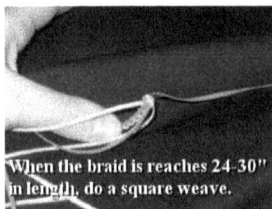

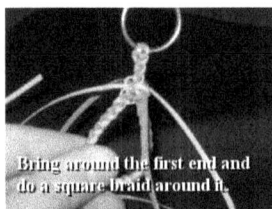

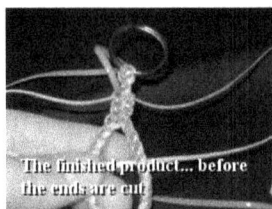

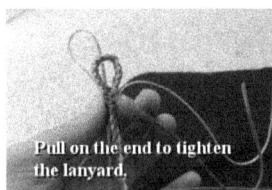

Start by choosing your favorite colors of paracord.

Tuningpeg571, CC BY-SA 3.0 <https://creativecommons.org/licenses/by-sa/3.0>, via Wikimedia Commons: https://commons.wikimedia.org/wiki/File:Lanyard.png

Step 1: Select Colors

Choose your favorite colors of paracord. Cut a length of cord, about 4 feet long, for a standard-sized keychain.

Step 2: Create a Cow Hitch Knot

Fold the cord in half, creating a loop. Pass the folded end through the key ring, then pull the loose ends through the loop, securing the cord to the ring.

Step 3: Begin Braiding

Separate the cords into two sets, each with two strands. Start braiding by using a simple, three-strand braid until you reach the desired length.

Step 4: Tie off the End

Once the braid is long enough, tie off the end with a knot. Trim any excess cord, leaving a small tail.

Step 5: Finishing Touch

Attach a key ring or lobster clasp to the looped end, and your personalized keychain is ready!

Lanyard

Step 1: Choose Colors

Select your favorite lanyard cord colors. Cut two pieces of cord, each about 5 feet long for a standard lanyard.

Step 2: Secure the Cords

Tie the two cords together at one end, creating a loop. This will be the top of your lanyard.

Step 3: Start a Box Stitch

Separate the cords into two pairs. Cross the left pair over the right pair, creating an "X." Pass the left pair behind the right pair.

Step 4: Continue the Box Stitch

Repeat the box stitch pattern, alternating left and right, until you reach the desired length.

Step 5: Finish and Attach a Swivel Clasp

Tie off the ends with a secure knot. Attach a swivel clasp to the looped end. Your colorful lanyard is now ready for use!

Zipper Pull

Step 1: Choose Cord and Colors

Select a vibrant color for your zipper pull. Cut a shorter length, around 2 feet, as zipper pulls don't need to be too long.

Step 2: Create a Cow Hitch Knot

Fold the cord in half and pass the folded end through the zipper pull or clip. Pull the loose ends through the loop, securing the cord.

Step 3: Add Beads (Optional)

Slide colorful beads onto the two loose ends to add a decorative touch.

Step 4: Tie a Knot

Tie a secure knot at the end of the cord, ensuring that the beads are held in place.

Step 5: Attach to Zipper

Attach the looped end to the zipper of a backpack, jacket, or any item with a zipper. Now, your zipper has a personalized and vibrant pull!

Experiment with different knotting techniques, colors, and bead arrangements to create truly unique and personalized accessories. This hands-on activity enhances crafting skills and instills a sense of pride in customizing your belongings.

The Art of Macramé

Macramé is a versatile and ancient craft that involves creating intricate and decorative patterns by using knotting techniques. The art of macramé has a rich history, with its roots dating back centuries, notably flourishing during the 13th-century Arab weavers and 17th-century European sailors. In recent years, macramé has experienced a resurgence in popularity as a creative and therapeutic outlet.

Basic Macramé Knots

Square Knot

This is one of the fundamental knots that is formed by overlapping two sets of cords. It is used to create flat or spiral patterns, and it is often seen in plant hangers and wall hangings.

Half Hitch Knot

This knot is created by wrapping one cord around another. It can be used for textured and linear designs, adding depth to macramé projects.

Lark's Head Knot

The Lark's Head knot is simple, and it is commonly used to attach cords to a dowel or a ring. It serves as the starting point for many macramé projects, such as wall hangings.

Double Half Hitch Knot

This one is similar to the half hitch, but it involves two consecutive wraps around the core cord. It creates a denser and more secure knot, and it is ideal for shaping and structure.

Popular Macramé Projects

From curtains to table runners, macramé can be used to adorn various home items.
Mimidellaboheme, CC BY-SA 4.0 <https://creativecommons.org/licenses/by-sa/4.0>, via Wikimedia Commons:
https://commons.wikimedia.org/wiki/File:Alberello_in_macram%C3%A9.jpg

Wall Hangings

Elaborate designs are created by combining various knots and patterns. Incorporate different materials, colors, and textures for a visually stunning result.

Plant Hangers

Utilize a combination of square knots and half hitch knots to form a cradle for holding plants. This is a stylish way to display greenery and add a bohemian touch to interiors.

Macramé Jewelry

Create intricate bracelets, necklaces, and earrings by using micro-macramé techniques. Incorporate beads and gemstones to enhance the aesthetics.

Home Décor

From curtains to table runners, macramé can be used to adorn various home items. It can be customizable to match different interior styles and color schemes.

Therapeutic Benefits of Macramé

Mindfulness and Focus

Macramé requires concentration on knotting patterns, promoting mindfulness and focus. It serves as a meditative practice, allowing individuals to be present in the creative process.

Stress Relief

Engaging in macramé provides a constructive and relaxing way to alleviate stress. The repetitive nature of knotting can have a calming effect on the mind.

Sense of Accomplishment

Completing a macramé project, whether large or intricate, instills a sense of achievement. It boosts self-esteem and encourages individuals to explore more complex patterns.

Creative Expression

Macramé allows for endless creative expression through the choice of knots, colors, and materials. Individuals can personalize their projects, resulting in unique and meaningful creations.

Whether you're a beginner or an experienced crafter, the art of macramé offers a wide range of possibilities for creating beautiful and functional items. With its therapeutic benefits and the satisfaction of producing handmade pieces, macramé continues to captivate crafters and enthusiasts worldwide.

Section 8: Tips and Tricks

Did you learn how to tie different types of knots? Great work! Now, the question remains: how fast can you tie one? Imagine you are sailing in a raft you helped build. When floating midwater, you notice two of the logs aren't tied properly, and the knots are rapidly opening up. You need to think fast and work your hands faster still. You need to re-tie the knot before the logs separate and disturb the balance of your raft.

In such a case of crisis, you don't have time to go through each knot-tying step methodically. You should think on your feet and tie the first knot that comes to mind as quickly as you can. Here are a few good tips to help you on your way to becoming a knot-tying master.

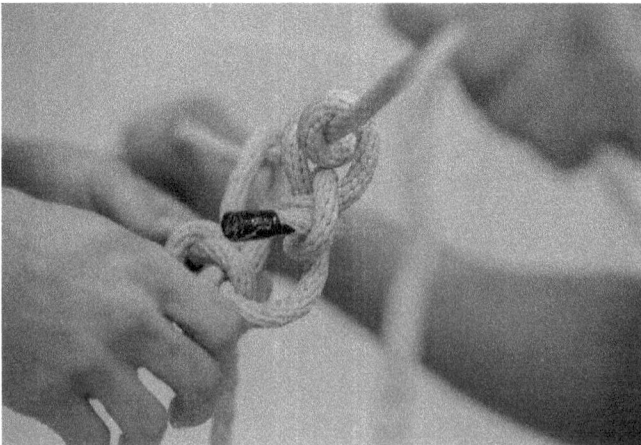

Practice tying knots.

- Practice, then practice some more! Rarely is anyone a knot-tying prodigy. Once you have acquired this essential skill, you should keep practicing it until you can tie the hardest knots quickly. For instance, the fisherman's knot may take several minutes to tie the first few times. As you practice, you will find that your hands will be getting used to the motions, and your mind will be able to picture the future steps well beforehand, helping you tie faster. You can even reduce the tying time to a minute or two with enough practice.

- Practice the simple knots first. With each simple knot you tie successfully, and as fast as you can, you will develop a healthy interest in the art. By the time you reach the complicated knots (the nautical knots, in particular), you will have learned to enjoy the entire process, from understanding the motions and alignments to pulling and tightening the rope. It won't remain a chore anymore but transform into an entertaining activity.

- Prevent fraying with scotch tape. Say you need to divide a single, long coil of rope into four short lengths to pitch a tent. When you cut the rope with a pair of scissors, the resulting two ends will be frayed like Albert Einstein's hair. The knots you tie with these may not be strong enough to hold your tent. Here's a simple trick to prevent fraying.

    1. Wrap the section of the rope you want to cut with scotch tape. One to two rounds of tape will be enough.
    2. Cut with scissors from the middle of the wrap.

This way, the resulting ends will be neatly cut without any threads sticking out.

- Don't dismiss the overhand knot. In the fascinating world of knots, the most fundamental knot in the world is easy to ignore. Despite being the simplest knot to tie, it can be alarmingly difficult to untie when the tension is too high. It's not among the most secure knots either. However, as you might know by now, without the overhand knot, you cannot tie many other types of knots (like the reef knot, the fisherman's knot, the angle loop, etc.) Plus, when you need to tie a knot fast, like when your raft is failing, you can use an overhand knot and take your time to create a sturdier knot.

- Understand the pros and cons of any knot. While you can secure yourself better to a climbing harness with a double bowline, it can be dangerous if you get it wrong. A figure-eight knot is much easier and safer to tie. Go through the pros and cons of each type of knot before experimenting with it in a real-world setting.
- Carry knot-tying tools. If you haven't practiced your knots enough before heading to the great outdoors, carrying a knot-tying tool, like a Marline Spike or a specially crafted knife would be beneficial. They will speed up the process of tying many kinds of knots.

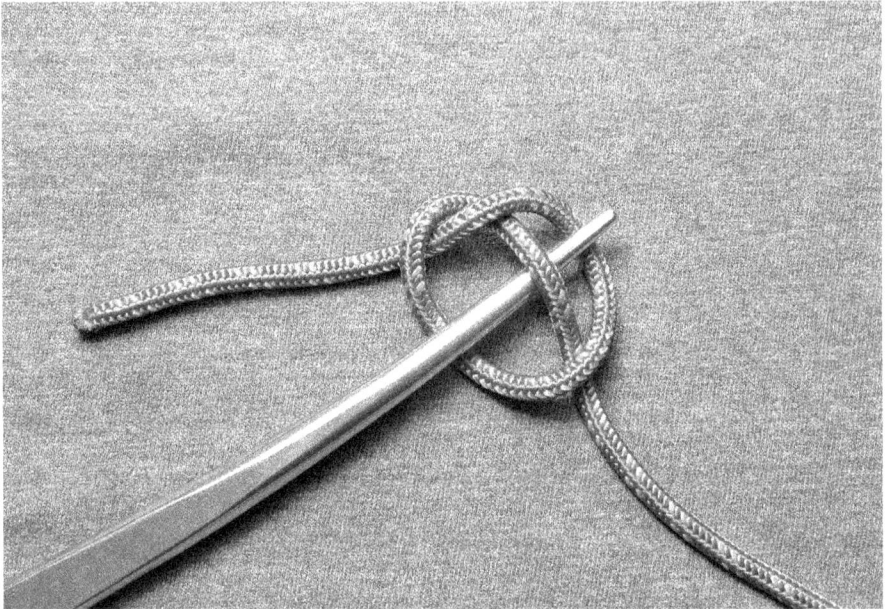

Carry knot-tying tools.

Useful Variations and Handy Shortcuts

Tying the most complicated knots is possible with practice, but doing the same hand motions and rope inserts over and over again can become boring. That is when the following interesting variations and handy shortcuts act like a breath of fresh air. (Show each of the knots below)

Braided Square Knot

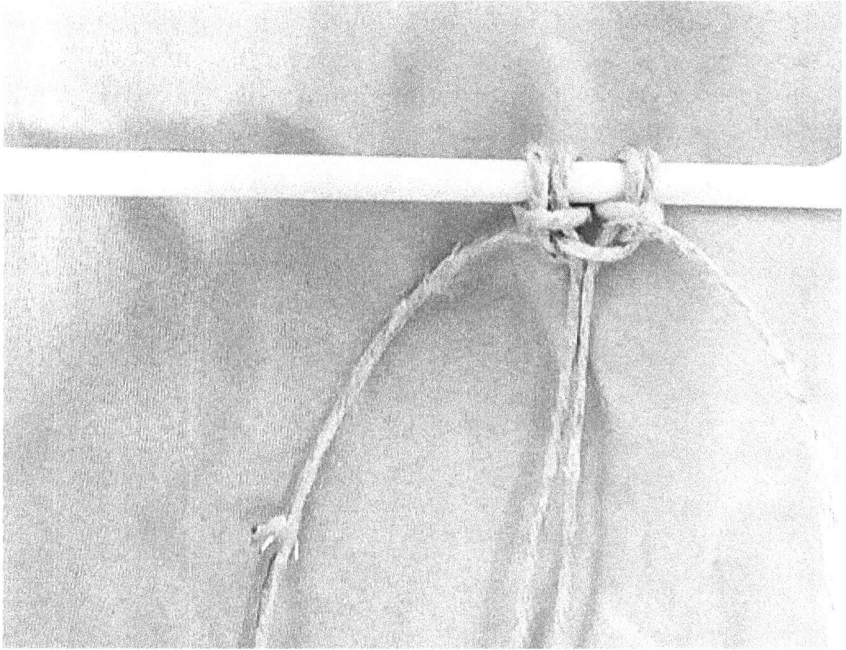

This is a fun way to practice tying a square knot.

This is a fun way to practice tying a square knot. At the end of this activity, you will end up with an attractive braid, just like a perfectly woven ponytail. You will need two ropes for this.

1. Tie the ropes to a rod with a Lark's Head knot (fold the rope in half, wrap it once around the rod, and insert both ends through the loop).

2. Bring them close together.

3. Hold the leftmost cord above the two middle cords and below the rightmost cord.

4. Bring the rightmost cord from under the middle cords and over (and through) the leftmost cord.

5. Pull the two ends to make a square knot that looks as if it's leaning slightly to the right.

6. Do the same, starting with the leftmost cord, then keep alternating.

You will get great practice in tying a square knot with both your hands. The more loops you complete, the better your rope braid will look.

Spiral Square Knot

Wish to transform your knots' sequence into a beautiful spiral design? For the braided knot, you alternated between the rightmost and the leftmost cords. To make a spiral out of it, you need to keep tying either a right-sided or a left-sided square knot. The more you tie, the more it will curve. If it's long enough, it will look like a spiraling strand of DNA!

Monkey's Fist

Monkey's Fist knot acts as a stopper to prevent the rope from slipping beyond the edge.

Markwell, CC BY-SA 3.0 <https://creativecommons.org/licenses/by-sa/3.0>, via Wikimedia Commons: https://commons.wikimedia.org/wiki/File:Paracord_monkey_fist.JPG

After tying your favorite knot, do those ugly little frayed ends of the rope bother you? You can cover them up with a cool, decorative knot called a Monkey's Fist. It also acts as a stopper to prevent the rope from slipping beyond the edge.

1. Wrap the rope end three times around two fingers of your left hand. Keep the fingers apart.

2. Wrap it horizontally between your fingers around the first wrapped loop.

3. Carefully pull out the structure, then insert the end through the center of the first loop and wrap it around the second loop. Do this twice more.

4. Tighten the cords by pulling the loops. The ends will emerge through the center. Put them back in to complete your Monkey's Fist.

The Bowline Shortcut

The bowline knot is one of the most useful knots in your repertoire. From anchoring boats to tying two ropes together, it has some of the best uses in the world of knot tying. However, the standard way of tying a bowline can be confusing for many. Here's a handy shortcut that will make the process easy.

1. Hold the rope in your left hand and make a loop in the middle (like turning the page of a book).

2. With your right hand, insert the top cord through the bottom of the loop. Hold it with your left hand as if to make an archway.

3. Take the rightmost end in your right hand and insert it into the archway from the left side.

4. Hold the end, along with the new loop, in your right hand and pull the alignment with both hands to tighten your bowline.

Improve your Cognitive Abilities with Exciting Activities

It is a proven theory that practicing knot-tying every day improves your cognitive abilities. Many of your cognitive skills come into action when you go through each step of tying knots.

- **Spatial Contextual Awareness:** Do you find it hard to judge the distance between two objects without using measuring tools? Do you tend to see the world in two dimensions instead of perceiving a three-dimensional space?

- **Motor Skills:** Do you find it hard to write anything? Is it tough for you to hold a pair of scissors?

- **Problem Solving:** Do you tend to come up with solutions that aren't effective? Do you make the same mistakes over and over again?

- **Memorizing:** Is it hard for you to remember simple things, like your close friend's hobbies or your mother's workplace?

All these skills will improve tenfold if you practice knot-tying regularly. The coordination between your fingers will become more refined, your memory will be as sharp as a tack, and you will start finding several effective solutions (not just one!) to your problems.

Nevertheless, is knot-tying too boring for you? Here are a few exciting activities that will keep you engaged in the art.

Knot-Tying Contest

You can play this with family or friends. Print pictures of all the finished knots shown in this book without the steps leading to them. The host will pick any picture randomly. You and the other competitors will have to recreate the knot shown. The one who finishes first will get one point. If your competitors aren't as good at knot tying as you are, then show the beginner's knots first, like the overhand and the figure-eight knots.

After playing this contest a few times, you will notice a healthy improvement in your memory and problem-solving abilities.

Friendship Bracelets

Do you want to surprise your friend with a gift or make new friends? Give them a cool, handmade friendship bracelet! You will need a 20-inch-long nylon cord – no more than two millimeters thick. You will also need to practice the sliding knot.

1. Hold the cord in a circular loop.
2. Make three smaller loops, with one end of the cord around the other end.
3. Insert the first end through the loops and tighten it.
4. Pull one end of the knot to slide a long length of the cord out (around 5 to 10 inches).
5. Tie another sliding knot on the diagonally opposite end of the first knot.

Depending on your friend's wrist, they can pull on either of the knots to loosen the bracelet or fasten it tight. If you are strapped for time, you can tie off the bracelet with a single sliding knot.

Simon Says What-Knot

This fun variation of Simon Says will test your problem-solving skills, retention, and attention span. The host will say, "Simon says...," with any type of knot. You will have to tie that knot in... say, two minutes. It will be *a miss* if you fail to tie the knot within the given time. After three misses, you will be out of the game.

If the host has only mentioned the knot without saying, "Simon says," then whoever begins to tie the knot will get a miss. Don't interrupt them just yet. Let them finish tying and see the look on their face when it's declared a miss!

Thank You

Knot tying might seem challenging at first (especially if learning new things by doing them isn't your favorite way to learn), but you've done a great job by using this book to help you! Now that you know the basic knots, you have a super cool skill you can use daily. You can turn this skill into a fun hobby, a neat craft, spice up your outdoor adventures, or just get things done faster.

Every new skill you learn makes you even more awesome. Getting good at important skills helps you be more independent, and you'll be glad for it as you grow. Remember, tying knots isn't just about making a perfect loop or twist; it's about figuring out solutions to tricky problems. Learning different knots means you're also learning to tackle tough situations.

If some knots don't work out right away, no sweat! It's all part of learning. Keep practicing; you'll be a knot-tying wizard before you know it.

Thanks for sticking with it, and congrats on finishing this book! Keep it handy for all your future knot-tying quests.

Here's another book by Dion Rosser that you might like

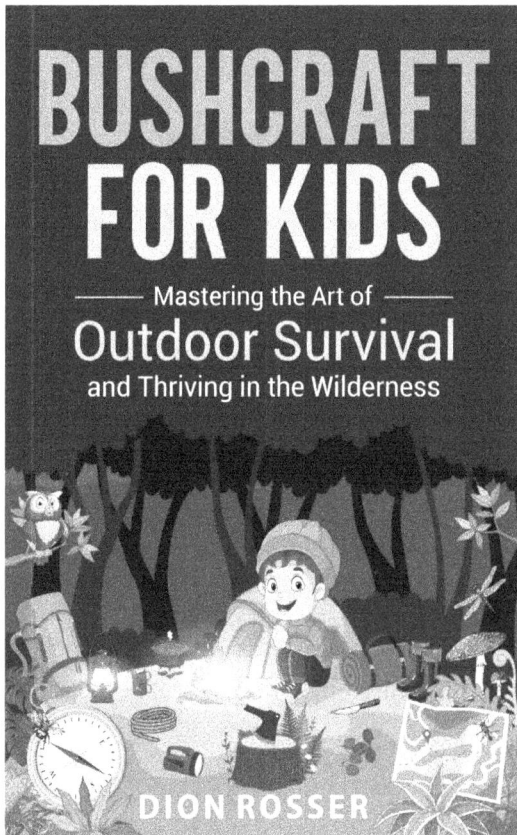

References

A beginner's guide to wilderness and backcountry hiking prep. (2015, July 23). National Park Foundation; #creator. https://www.nationalparks.org/connect/blog/beginners-guide-wilderness-backcountry-hiking-prep

Low, R. (2022, November 16). How to plan a multi-day outdoor adventure. Adventure Treks. https://www.adventuretreks.com/blog/multi-day-adventure/

Mentor, C. (2020, March 25). 5 basic survival skills. Wilderness Awareness School. https://wildernessawareness.org/articles/5-basic-survival-skills/

Pinkston, J. (2021, January 5). Teaching Kids Survival Skills. Don't Die In The Woods. https://dontdieinthewoods.com/blogs/survival-skills/teaching-kids-survival-skills

Pisner, J. (2020, November 11). 13 steps to plan a backpacking trip. Backhacker Babe. https://www.backhackerbabe.com/blog/13-steps-to-plan-a-backpacking-trip

Skurka, A. (2020, July 8). How to plan a successful backpacking trip in 7 steps. Outside Online. https://www.outsideonline.com/outdoor-adventure/hiking-and-backpacking/how-to-plan-backpacking-trip/

Steinberg, B. (2021, January 28). A guide to safe & effective planning for trips into the wilderness. Silent Sports. https://silentsportsmagazine.com/2021/01/28/a-guide-to-safe-effective-planning-for-trips-into-the-wilderness/

(N.d.-a). Rei.com. https://www.rei.com/learn/expert-advice/backpack-planning.html

(N.d.-b). Veggievagabonds.com. https://veggievagabonds.com/adventure-planning/

Anderberg, J. (2016, April 20). How to find water in the wild. The Art of Manliness; Art of Manliness. https://www.artofmanliness.com/skills/outdoor-survival/how-to-find-water-in-the-wild/

Bennett, J. (2016, December 8). Everything you need to know about foraging for food in the wild. Popular Mechanics. https://www.popularmechanics.com/adventure/outdoors/tips/a24203/eat-forage-food-wild-alone-history-channel/

Bryant, C. W. (2021, April 9). How to find water in the wild. MapQuest Travel. https://www.mapquest.com/travel/survival/wilderness/how-to-find-water.htm

Dandelions for your salad. (n.d.). Eatright.org. https://www.eatright.org/food/food-groups/vegetables/dandelions-for-your-salad

DNews. (2011, November 4). Top ways to purify water in the wilderness. Seeker. https://www.seeker.com/top-ways-to-purify-water-in-the-wilderness-1765491027.html

Foraging for wild edibles: A practical approach. (n.d.). Alderleaf Wilderness College. https://www.wildernesscollege.com/foraging-for-wild-edibles.html

How to find water in the wilderness. (2018, October 19). Bushcraft Buddy. https://bushcraftbuddy.com/how-to-find-water-in-the-wilderness/

Jones, B. (2018, August 3). A beginner's guide to finding wild edible plants that won't kill you. Popular Science. https://www.popsci.com/find-wild-edible-plants/

Naranjo, N. (2023, May 12). A camper's guide to water containers and safe drinking solutions. LuminAID. https://luminaid.com/blogs/news/camping-water-containers

Schauf, C. (2018, September 27). How to purify water in the wild. Uncharted Supply Company. https://unchartedsupplyco.com/blogs/news/purify-water-in-wild

Seitz, D. (2020, February 5). How to find drinkable water in the wild. Popular Science. https://www.popsci.com/story/diy/find-drinkable-water-wild/

Two ways to purify water (U.S. National Park service). (n.d.). Nps.gov. https://www.nps.gov/articles/2wayspurifywater.htm

Williams, T. (2023, June 27). Your Survival Guide on how to find Water in the Wilderness. Desert Island Survival. https://www.desertislandsurvival.com/how-to-find-water/

(N.d.-a). Masterclass.com. https://www.masterclass.com/articles/universal-edibility-test

(N.d.-b). Masterclass.com. https://www.masterclass.com/articles/foraging-guide

(N.d.-c). Masterclass.com. https://www.masterclass.com/articles/how-to-find-water

3 things a fire needs - frontier fire protection. (n.d.). Frontierfireprotection.com. https://www.frontierfireprotection.com/3-things-fire-needs/

5 precautions to keep your bonfire or campfire safe. (2016, September 28). Fbfs.com. https://www.fbfs.com/learning-center/5-precautions-to-keep-your-bonfire-or-campfire-safe

Crew, C. (2021, October 12). How to make a campfire and leave no trace. Campsited. https://www.campsited.com/en/blog/how-to-make-a-campfire-and-leave-no-trace/

Edelen, B. (2007, December 19). 6 ways to make fire without matches or a lighter. WikiHow. https://www.wikihow.com/Make-Fire-Without-Matches-or-a-Lighter

Forest Survival Information. (2021, July 5). How to find dry firewood. Forest Info. https://forestinfo.org/how-to-find-dry-firewood/

Lean-to fire - the best way to build A campfire? (n.d.). Firewood For Life. https://www.firewood-for-life.com/lean-to-fire.html

Log Cabin Fire. (n.d.). Firewood For Life. https://www.firewood-for-life.com/log-cabin-fire.html

London, S. (2013, April 25). Back to basics with the fire triangle. Scutum London. https://www.scutumlondon.co.uk/help-advice/basics-fire-triangle/

Outdoor skills: Teaching kids how to build A fire & fire safety tips. (2021, March 8). RUN WILD MY CHILD. https://runwildmychild.com/building-fires-kids/

Teepee Fire. (n.d.). Firewood For Life. https://www.firewood-for-life.com/teepee-fire.html

Top 10 tips for campfire safety. (n.d.). Reserveamerica.com. https://www.reserveamerica.com/articles/camping/top-10-tips-for-campfire-safety

Barber, B. (2023, March 17). 7 most important tarp knots to know. Mom Goes Camping. https://momgoescamping.com/tarp-knots/

Higgins, D. (n.d.). How to build a shelter. Youngnaturalistsclub.com. http://youngnaturalistsclub.com/2020/05/15/how-to-build-a-shelter/

Master, F. (2023, May 12). The silent threat: 5 tips on how to identify A dead tree. Forest Master. https://forest-master.com/2023/05/12/5-tips-on-how-to-identify-a-dead-tree/

Survival skills challenge: Building a shelter. (2017, July 31). There's Just One Mommy. https://theresjustonemommy.com/survival-skills-challenge-building-a-shelter/

(N.d.). Blm.gov. https://www.blm.gov/sites/default/files/documents/files/Learn_CCSC_Nature-Learning-Downloads_Shelter-Building.pdf

Buchholz, R. (2021, May 3). How to get kids to respect wildlife. Family. https://www.nationalgeographic.com/family/article/respect-wildlife

Common Raccoon (Procyon lotor). (n.d.). https://tpwd.texas.gov/huntwild/wild/species/raccoon/

Coyote: Mammals: Species Information: Wildlife: Fish & Wildlife: Maine Dept of Inland Fisheries and Wildlife. (n.d.). https://www.maine.gov/ifw/fish-wildlife/wildlife/species-information/mammals/coyote.html

Dragoo, J. (2023, October 3). Skunk | Scent, Size, Habitat, & Facts. Encyclopedia Britannica. https://www.britannica.com/animal/skunk

Hiking Etiquette (U.S. National Park Service). (n.d.). https://www.nps.gov/articles/hikingetiquette.htm

Information on Common Wildlife Species | Westford, MA. (n.d.). https://westfordma.gov/151/Information-on-Common-Wildlife-Species

Leave No Trace. (2023, July 2). Principle 6: Respect Wildlife - Leave No Trace. https://lnt.org/why/7-principles/respect-wildlife/

Leave No Trace - Respect Wildlife. (n.d.). https://www.leavenotracedude.com/respect-wildlife.php

Oceans2Earth, & Oceans2Earth. (2022). Why we need to show animals kindness and respect. Oceans2Earth. https://oceans2earth.org/why-we-need-to-show-animals-kindness-and-respect/

Squirrels 101: Facts, Photos & Information on Squirrels. (n.d.). https://www.pestworld.org/news-hub/pest-articles/squirrels-101/

Staying Safe Around Bears - Bears (U.S. National Park Service). (n.d.). https://www.nps.gov/subjects/bears/safety.htm

Tim Knight - University of Washington. (n.d.). American Black Bear Facts for Kids - NatureMapping. http://naturemappingfoundation.org/natmap/facts/american_black_bear_k6.html

What to Do if You Encounter a Coyote | City of Edmonton. (n.d.). https://www.edmonton.ca/residential_neighbourhoods/pets_wildlife/what-to-do-if-you-encounter-a-coyote

White-Tailed Deer - WildlifeNYC. (n.d.). https://www.nyc.gov/site/wildlifenyc/animals/deer.page

Brown, T., & Morgan, A. B., Jr. (2023, April 4). Making cordage from natural materials. Mother Earth News – The Original Guide To Living Wisely; Mother Earth News. https://www.motherearthnews.com/diy/making-cordage-natural-materials-zmaz83jfzraw/

(2006, July 4). 3 ways to make a spear. WikiHow. https://www.wikihow.com/Make-a-Spear

How to make a fishing spear. (n.d.). Hedgehog Leatherworks. https://hedgehogleatherworks.com/blogs/blog/how-to-make-a-fishing-spear

Making survival traps. (2020, May 11). The Survival University. https://thesurvivaluniversity.com/survival-tips/wilderness-survival-tips/survival-traps/

O'Dea, M. (2023, September 27). 14 wilderness survival tools you should always have in your pack. The Dyrt Magazine. https://thedyrt.com/magazine/gear/wilderness-survival-tools/

Primitive Stone Tools. (n.d.). Alderleaf Wilderness College. https://www.wildernesscollege.com/primitive-stone-tools.html

Wilderness Arena. (2015, December 31). How to build primitive weapons and tools from natural bone, rocks, shells, antlers, or animal teeth - geek. Geek Slop. https://www.geekslop.com/life/survival/tools-supplies/2015/how-to-build-primitive-weapons-and-tools-from-natural-bone-rocks-shells-antlers-or-animal-teeth

Bites and stings – first aid. (n.d.). Gov.au. https://www.betterhealth.vic.gov.au/health/healthyliving/bites-and-stings-first-aid

Camping and hiking first aid kits. (n.d.). Elastoplast.co.uk. https://www.elastoplast.co.uk/did-you-know/health-and-protection/camping-and-hiking-first-aid-kit

Children's Health. (n.d.). Snake bites and children: What to do. Childrens.com. https://www.childrens.com/health-wellness/snake-bites-and-children-what-to-do

How to handle an emergency. (n.d.). Kidshealth.org. https://kidshealth.org/en/kids/emergency.html

Omohundro, N. (2021, May 20). DIY outdoor first aid kit & checklist. Little Family Adventure. https://littlefamilyadventure.com/diy-outdoor-first-aid-kit-checklist/

Aga, & Aga. (2018). How To Mark Trails Like A Pro. American Gun Association. https://blog.gunassociation.org/mark-trails-like-pro/

Dempsey, C. (2021). How to Read a Map. GIS Lounge. https://www.gislounge.com/making-maps-easier-to-read/

Direction. (n.d.). https://education.nationalgeographic.org/resource/direction/

McKay, B. K. (2021). How to Find Direction Using the Sun and Stars. The Art of Manliness. https://www.artofmanliness.com/skills/outdoor-survival/find-direction-without-compass/

Notes on Cardinal Directions. (2022, July 20). Unacademy. https://unacademy.com/content/cat/study-material/data-interpretation-and-logical-reasoning/cardinal-directions/

10 Household Items That Can Double as Survival Gear. (n.d.). Mossy Oak. https://www.mossyoak.com/our-obsession/blogs/10-household-items-that-can-double-as-survival-gear

10 secrets of successful wildlife watching — WildSweden - wildlife adventures in Sweden. (n.d.). WildSweden - Wildlife Adventures in Sweden. https://www.wildsweden.com/about/10-secrets-of-successful-wildlife-watching

John. (2023, May 7). Get Prepared: How to Survive When Lost in The Wilderness? Tactical Backpacks and Military Gears! https://www.tacticalogy.com/lost-in-wilderness-survival-guide/

Observing Wildlife | Wildlife Journal Junior. (n.d.). https://nhpbs.org/wild/observing.asp

ReadyWise. (n.d.). Staying Calm in Emergencies. ReadyWise. https://readywise.com/blogs/readywise-blog/staying-calm-in-emergencies

Signaling | Be Ready Utah. (n.d.). https://beready.utah.gov/family-preparedness/12-areas-of-preparedness/communication/signaling/

Survival psychology | Meaning, Definition, Origin. (n.d.). Survival Kompass. https://survival-kompass.de/dictionary/survival-psychology/

Top 10 Outdoor Survival Skills and Hacks. (n.d.). https://www.reserveamerica.com/articles/hiking/top-10-outdoor-survival-skills-and-hacks

101 Knots. (n.d.). Decorative Knots. 101Knots. https://www.101knots.com/category/decorative-knots

101 Knots. (2017, August 4). How to Tie a Granny Knot? Tips, Variations, Uses & Video Steps. 101Knots. https://www.101knots.com/granny-knot.html

Animated Knots. (n.d.-a). Basic Knots. Www.animatedknots.com. https://www.animatedknots.com/basic-knots

Animated Knots. (n.d.-b). Half Hitch Knot. Www.animatedknots.com. https://www.animatedknots.com/half-hitch-knot

Animated Knots. (2019a). Overhand Knot. Animatedknots.com. https://www.animatedknots.com/overhand-knot

Animated Knots. (2019b, February 26). Two Half Hitches. Www.animatedknots.com. https://www.animatedknots.com/two-half-hitches-knot

Avonturier, D. van een. (2020, June 27). Essential Knots for Camping, Hiking and Survival. Dagboek van Een Avonturier. https://dagboekvaneenavonturier.com/2020/06/27/essential-knots-for-camping-hiking-and-survival/

Canyon Guides International. (n.d.). The science behind teaching & learning: Tying Knots – Canyon Guides International. Canyon Guides International. https://canyonguidesinternational.org/the-science-behind-teaching-learning-tying-knots/

Casadella, N. (2023, June 5). 13 Basic Macrame Knots: A Guide For Beginners. GANXXET. https://www.ganxxet.com/blogs/news/macrame-knots

Chest of Books. (n.d.). Decorative Knots. Chestofbooks.com. https://chestofbooks.com/crafts/camping/Creative/Decorative-Knots.html

Dave. (2019, May 6). 6 Important Knots You Should Know. Copake Camping Resort. https://copakecampingresort.com/6-important-knots-you-should-know/

Davidson, L. (2018, September 7). Useful Tips, Terms, and Techniques for Knot Tying - Grit. Www.grit.com. https://www.grit.com/tools/useful-tips-terms-techniques-knot-tying-ze0z1809zmcg/

Dean, T. (2016, May 27). How to Tie a Bow Tie: Easy Step-by-Step Video. Theknot.com. https://www.theknot.com/content/how-to-tie-a-bow-tie

Digital, P. (2022, July 22). Rope materials: a beginner's guide - RopesDirect. Ropes Direct. https://www.ropesdirect.co.uk/blog/rope-materials-a-beginners-guide-to-different-types-of-rope/

Discover Boating. (n.d.). 5 Ways to Bring Learning Onboard for the Kids This Summer. Discover Boating. https://www.discoverboating.com/resources/learning-onboard-a-boat

Flashman, J. (2021, April 21). What's the Best Tie-in Knot? The Bowline vs. The Figure 8 Knot. Climbing. https://www.climbing.com/skills/tying-in-the-bowline-vs-the-figure-8-knot/

Fouche, M. (2023, August 4). 8 Basic Survival Knots You Should Know. SkyAboveUs. https://skyaboveus.com/wilderness-survival/8-Essential-Knots-You-Should-Know-Survival-Skills

Fury, S. (n.d.). 8 Basic Knots and Their Uses. Www.survivalfitnessplan.com. https://www.survivalfitnessplan.com/blog/basic-knots-and-their-uses

Gawlikowski, G. (2016, November 9). 17 Essential Knots Every Survivalist Needs to Know. ROFFSTM. https://roffs.com/2016/11/17-essential-knots-every-survivalist-needs-know/

House, M. (2019, February 27). Six of the Most Useful Outdoor & Survival Knots You Should Know. Mountain House. https://mountainhouse.com/blogs/emergency-prep-survival/six-of-the-most-useful-outdoor-survival-knots-you-should-know

Jessyratfink. (n.d.). How to Make a Friendship Bracelet. Instructables. https://www.instructables.com/how-to-make-a-friendship-bracelet-1/

Keech, K. (2023, February 14). What Are Knots? The History and Uses. Www.theknotsmanual.com. https://www.theknotsmanual.com/knots/

Kenninger, M. (2020, February 18). History of Knots and Common Uses. Rope and Cord. https://ropeandcord.com/guides-ideas/history-of-knots-and-common-uses/

Kilpatrick, T. (2023, May 25). Securing a bundle of wood, lashing up a backpack, or just tying your shoes, the square knot is essential. The Manual. https://www.themanual.com/outdoors/how-to-tie-a-square-knot/

Knotter. (2013, July 4). Tools Used for Knotting. Solent Branch. https://igkt-solent.co.uk/knotting-tools/

Luke. (2019, February 14). A Selective History of Knots and Rope. Paracord Planet. https://www.paracordplanet.com/blog/a-selective-history-of-knots-and-rope/

Lund, T., & Garbacz, A. (2023, October 2). 4 Ways to Tie a Knot. WikiHow. https://www.wikihow.com/Tie-a-Knot

Net Knots. (n.d.-a). Bowline on a Bight - How to tie a Bowline on a Bight. Www.netknots.com. https://www.netknots.com/rope_knots/bowline-on-a-bight

Net Knots. (n.d.-b). Harness Bend Knot | How to tie a Harness Bend | All knots animated. Www.netknots.com. https://www.netknots.com/rope_knots/harness-bend

Net Knots. (n.d.-c). Slip Knot - How to tie a Slip Knot. Www.netknots.com. https://www.netknots.com/rope_knots/slip-knot

NUCC. (2022, April 12). Rigging Knots. Nucc.caves.org.au. https://nucc.caves.org.au/detailedsrt/knot/

Raleigh, D. (2022, February 15). Essential Climbing Knots — The Complete Guide. Climbing. https://www.climbing.com/skills/essential-climbing-knots-complete-guide/

Ribbins, A. (2023, August 11). Sailing Knots For Beginners Complete Guide. UKSA. https://uksa.org/sailing-knots-for-beginners-guide/

Riddle, T. C. (n.d.). Knots for Everyday Use — Texas Parks & Wildlife Department. Tpwd.texas.gov. https://tpwd.texas.gov/calendar/bentsen-rio-grande-valley/knots-for-everyday-use

Royal Museums Greenwich. (n.d.-a). How to tie a bowline knot | Royal Museums Greenwich. Www.rmg.co.uk. https://www.rmg.co.uk/stories/topics/how-tie-bowline-knot

Royal Museums Greenwich. (n.d.-b). How to tie a round turn and two half hitches knot. Www.rmg.co.uk. https://www.rmg.co.uk/stories/topics/how-tie-round-turn-two-half-hitches-knot

Royal Museums Greenwich. (n.d.-c). How to tie a sheet bend knot | Royal Museums Greenwich. Www.rmg.co.uk. https://www.rmg.co.uk/stories/topics/how-tie-sheet-bend-knot

Sailing, A. (2022, November 29). How to Tie 3 Important Sailing Knots. American Sailing. https://asa.com/news/2022/11/29/sailing-knots/

Sikora, K. (2020, April 7). Learn How to Tie Basic Fishing Knots. Www.wheredoitakethekids.com. https://www.wheredoitakethekids.com/blog/fishing-knots/

Smothermon-Short, S. (2022, March 3). 10 Knot Tying Games for Cub Scouts. Cub Scout Ideas. https://cubscoutideas.com/20457/10-knot-tying-games-for-cub-scouts/

Stearns, S. (2023, March 8). 17 Basic Macrame Knots: Step-by-Step Instructions. Sarah Maker. https://sarahmaker.com/basic-macrame-knots/

Unitarian Universalist Association. (n.d.). Activity 2: Tying Sailor Knots | Love Connects Us | Tapestry of Faith | UUA.org. Www.uua.org. https://www.uua.org/re/tapestry/children/loveconnects/session5/161791.shtml